ENDORSEME(N)T

"The *You Are A Miracle Workbook* is an excellent book to start you on your healing journey from sexual abuse to wholeness. It includes many self-help techniques and exercises after each chapter that the reader can easily complete, thereby *allowing* you to realize and express feelings that may have been locked up. Reading this book will bring you to a closer relationship with Jesus because it is filled with scriptures and examples of what a good, kind and benevolent God we have, who wants to help us fulfill our road to recovery and remove the guilt and shame that so often is associated with sexual abuse. Samantha Thomas has managed to keep the workbook positive and uplifting for the reader even while delving into the difficult subject of childhood sexual abuse."
Survivor of Childhood Sexual Abuse, Midhurst, Ontario.

"*You Are A Miracle Workbook* is a dynamic self-help tool that intertwines Cognitive-Behavioural Therapy and Spirituality for the woman survivor of sexual abuse who is committed to healing and moving forward in her life. It offers hands-on practical techniques for women to work through their own personal healing journey."
LeeAnn Furlotte, BSW, RSW, MEdC, CCC

"*You Are A Miracle Workbook* is a 'must have' resource for professional counselors and their clients who have been victimized by the trauma of sexual abuse. Utilizing effective and practical Cognitive Behavioural Therapy (CBT) strategies, this ground-breaking curriculum gently integrates the therapeutic power of God's love into the journey to healing."
Hugh McIntosh, Senior Counselor www.menofvalour.org

Child sexual trauma can challenge and devastate that which is most sacred: our innocence, our faith and trust in God. *You Are A Miracle Workbook* provides Christian survivors with an opportunity to deepen their understanding of the ways in which their abuse experience has affected their spiritual growth and shares concrete tools to begin the journey of rebuilding and restoring their relationship with God."
Nicole Tremblay M.S.W, R.S.W

People say we don't see miracles anymore, but this book "*You Are A Miracle Workbook*" will prove that statement wrong. This book shows God working through the author, Samantha Thomas to allow the healing process to begin by marrying God's love with traditional social work techniques. This book will bring about an amazing personal journey as one "peels away" the pain, shame and deep emotional hurt and go from being wounded to becoming a new creation in Christ Jesus.
Suzanne Rankin, Central Ontario

"...an easy read but powerfully written. *You Are A Miracle Workbook* specifically identifies the signs and symptoms of female sexual abuse. Working through the exercises will delicately guide victims of sexual abuse on their spiritual journey to be the MIRACLE God made them to be."
Katherine McIntosh, Registered Nurse

WORKBOOK

Restoring hope one
piece at a time

You
are a
Miracle

Rebuilding After
Childhood Sexual Abuse

Samantha Thomas, M.S.W., R.S.W.

YOU ARE A MIRACLE WORKBOOK:
Rebuilding After Childhood Sexual Abuse
Copyright © 2012 by Samantha Thoman M.S.W., R.S.W.

Scripture taken from the HOLY BIBLE, NEW INTERNATIONAL VERSION®. Copyright © 1973, 1978, 1984 International Bible Society. Used by permission of Zondervan. All rights reserved.

ISBN: 978-1-77069-678-5

Word Alive Press
131 Cordite Road, Winnipeg, MB R3W 1S1
www.wordalivepress.ca

Library and Archives Canada Cataloguing in Publication
Thomas, Samantha, 1973-
    You are a miracle workbook : rebuilding after childhood sexual abuse / Samantha Thomas.
ISBN 978-1-77069-678-5
    1. Adult child sexual abuse victims--Religious life. 2. Adult child sexual abuse victims--Rehabilitation. I. Title.
BL625.9.A37T56 2012   261.8'3272   C2012-904696-5

Acknowledgements

I dedicate this book to the millions of survivors of childhood sexual abuse.

I thank God for the opportunity and the privilege to share my work. For with Him, all is possible.

To my amazing husband, you are a gift sent by God. Thank you for loving me unconditionally through my healing journey. You were definitely Jesus' hands and feet during my valleys and stood with me on the top of the mountain. Thank you for holding my arms up during those moments I wanted to quit. You are a SOLID guy! I was able to achieve many things in life because of your consistent encouragement. Thank you for encouraging me to write this book. You were right — I'm writing for one audience -- God.

To my precious children, Isaac & Shaniqwa, you two are my greatest joy. May this book be a testament to both of you that with God's help all is possible!

To Mom, thank you for teaching me to love my children and being my greatest encourager! My prayer is that this book will help mothers who have experienced childhood sexual abuse. I pray mothers will look to Jesus for their healing so that they can be present in the lives of their children and give their children the love and guidance they deserve.

Thank you to my family, each of you have made a deposit of love into my life. May each of you reach your dreams that God has breathed into your spirit. You are highly favored!

Thank you to my colleagues and friends. A special gratitude to the pastors of Emmanuel Baptist Church in Barrie, Ontario! Thank you for your generosity in reading my manuscript, offering feedback and supporting me over the years.

A special thank you to my editor, Nancy Maisuria!

Table of Contents

MODULE FOUR—Emotions

Preface

"I learned this the hard way. For so long, I could not find any purpose in my pain. I never saw the beauty—I felt like all I had were the ashes. I was filled with shame over what I've done and anger over what had been done to me."

Joyce Meyer

SEXUAL VIOLENCE AGAINST WOMEN IS A SIGNIFICANT HEALTH ISSUE IN OUR SOCIETY. SEXUAL VIOLENCE includes, but is not limited to, childhood sexual abuse, molestation and rape. The relative risk for mental health problems resulting from experiencing sexual violence is different for every woman. Survivors of sexual violence often experience short-term and long-term effects, which can affect many areas of their lives, as well as families and communities. Women who have experienced the trauma of sexual abuse utilize diverse coping strategies. There is no right or wrong way of reacting to sexual abuse. However, you may develop patterns of coping that initially seem effective, but over time, these behaviours no longer serve your best interests and/or interfere with true satisfaction in life. If you are reading this book, it is no accident or coincidence. Are you struggling to experience real happiness in your life? Have you tried many things, which were ineffective to restore your joy? Well, this book is for you!

God placed this workbook on my heart to share with you the spiritual and therapeutic strategies He revealed to me. These strategies led to my own powerful healing journey and deepened my relationship with Him. This book is designed to give powerful spiritual strategies to heal you from your painful experiences. I believe it will provide you with practical strategies that will inspire and encourage you to lean on God, who will help you overcome the pain you are experiencing right now. As a survivor of sexual violence, I learned a vital lesson: to successfully heal from my painful experiences of sexual violence - I had to be conscious of God's presence and His unconditional love for me. Trusting in His unfailing love, I was able to become a new creature...no more depression, no more hatred toward others, no more shame, no more insecurities and most importantly, no more guilt. Due to the healing power of Jesus, I have seen many relationships restored, witnessed transformations in areas of my life and in the lives of other women with whom I have used these strategies. God is the source who can supply all my needs. I'm now free to be the person He created and desired me to be - fearfully and wonderfully made! I'm now excited about life and know that if you also apply these spiritual strategies to what you are experiencing right now, God will restore joy and hope in your life and ignite an amazing healing journey!

Samantha Thomas M.S.W., R.S.W
June 2, 2012

Introduction: Before You Start

THERE ARE VERY FEW SELF-HELP RESOURCES FOR WOMEN SURVIVORS OF CHILDHOOD SEXUAL ABUSE THAT incorporate spirituality into treatment. *You Are A Miracle Workbook* was written to address this need. It offers an understanding as well as specific tools for the process of healing based on the Christian faith that will instill hope for women survivors of childhood sexual abuse. The program you are about to embark upon is based on professional literature and empirical research on sexual abuse, Christian principles, my training and from my clinical work with survivors. This book is designed to help you cope in your present day-to-day life following the sexual abuse that you have experienced. To use this workbook you do not need to be a Christian but simply come with an open mind to learn strategies that will help you heal from the sexual violence that you have experienced and gain a deeper understanding of our powerful, generous, giving and compassionate God! You may have tried to maintain your faith and developed your spirituality to address the abuse, but you may still be experiencing a void or emptiness within your spirit. *You Are a Miracle Workbook* utilizes intervention strategies that will help build on your current spirituality and help you deepen your relationship with God so He can heal your hurts, restore hope in your life and fill that emptiness in your spirit with His love!

The exercise section asks you to think about your life right now. **You will not be asked to think about the sexual abuse itself or its details. Please do not use an incident of sexual abuse for any of the activities in this book.** You are not required to think about the details of the sexual abuse you experienced to prevent you from having an acute stress reaction. It is possible to heal from sexual abuse without focusing on the details of each incident of abuse. In this workbook, you will have the opportunity to complete numerous exercises that will give you insight into your symptoms, your beliefs, your behaviour and your feelings about the sexual abuse you endured. This book was written so you can use it on your own. If you desire, it can be used as part of the psychotherapy process. If you need more help than this book can offer, I encourage you to see a psychotherapist with specialized training in treating childhood sexual abuse. Much of the work of healing from sexual abuse is accomplished best with one or more supportive persons. Sexual abuse is very isolating and can leave you feeling disconnected from others. Sharing your healing journey with others can be very comforting. I encourage you to access the support of friends, family, Therapists, Pastors, church leaders and/or a support group. Sharing with supportive persons about how you feel and think will be helpful for your healing journey. If at any time during this process you feel triggered, emotionally distressed or unsure on how to move ahead, I strongly recommend that you find a counseling professional who is trained in the treatment of childhood sexual abuse.

How this book is organized:
This book has been set up into four different modules, which are designed to make it user-friendly.

1. **Education module** will give you an understanding of Childhood Sexual Abuse. In this section, you will find an initial assessment tool to examine how the sexual abuse you experienced may have impacted your spiritual development.

2. **Cognitive module** will require you to examine your thinking process. It is necessary to explore and understand how your thoughts impact your behaviour and feelings. You will learn valuable strategies to help you reframe and refocus your thoughts to promote emotional, physical and spiritual well-being.

3. **Behaviour module** will examine your current behaviour and help you to learn new strategies.

4. **Emotions module** will teach you how to identify, rate the intensity and learn ways to manage your own emotions. You will learn how all your emotions and body sensations are influenced or influence what you think and your behaviour.

The three main components (cognitive, behaviour and emotions) interconnect to form the basis of the Trauma Focused-Cognitive Behaviour Therapy approach which is underlying *You Are A Miracle Workbook*. The effectiveness of these tools will help you grow in your faith and strengthen your relationship with God, as long as you continue to depend on and commune with Jesus.

MODULEONE
Psychoeducation

Information About Childhood Sexual Abuse & Spirituality

CHAPTER ONE

Your Spiritual Development

Did you know that childhood sexual abuse can have significant, even detrimental effects on your spiritual development? Childhood sexual abuse has numerous negative effects on women. The severity and specific form of these effects vary with women over time. Women may experience significant psychological and emotional distress. The often ignored impact on women who have experienced childhood sexual abuse is on their spiritual development. We are spiritual beings. Ganje-Fling et al., (2000) suggests that the spiritual development of abuse victims is arrested or stopped at the age level at which the abuse occurs. Ganje-Fling and McCarthy (Dec 2011) report just as the psychological development of the survivor tends to be arrested around the age of abuse, so does the person's spiritual development. These researchers found spiritual concepts may have been underdeveloped, and the ability to acknowledge a spiritual source can be limited for survivors. Answers to existential questions such as life's meaning and purpose may be static, and the survivor may not be open to change in her concepts. Despair, mistrust, and low self-esteem are common impediments to a survivor's psychosocial functioning and her spiritual functioning (Ganje-Fling & McCarthy, Dec 2011). The impact of sexual abuse on spiritual develop is often ignored in treatment of survivors of sexual abuse. More participants than therapists reported raised spirituality topics in treatment (Ganje-Fling et al., Jan 2000).

Traditional healing/treatment practices encourage women to focus on personal development. However, traditional treatment practices that focus on personal development ignore the spiritual background of survivors and do not help to improve spiritual functioning. Whereas, personal development treatment encourages individuals to reduce stress in their lives, focus on career advancement, and to focus on developing hobbies such as pottery or gardening. Personal development treatment approaches to help survivors to function better in day to day life – personally or professionally. Unfortunately, personal development practices do not include spiritual development. Exclusion of spiritual development involves ignoring any reference to a higher power or God. Personal development treatment practices do not assist survivors to deepen their relationship with God nor acknowledge God as the ultimate healer of survivors.

Some survivors consciously decide that they are going to engage in personal development in the hope of healing from sexual abuse. Some women choose to purse spiritual growth to avoid personal development. Unless survivors address the spiritual development and their personal development, they will have limited healing.

The decision to pursue spiritual growth must be a conscious decision as it requires survivors to acknowledge God as having the transforming power to heal their lives. God's powers work with your faith to release healing in any area of your life that you need. When you look at your healing journey and treatment you have received to date---did you focus solely on personal development and neglect your spiritual development? Focusing solely on your personal development may lead to problems such as intensified feelings of loneliness or a feeling of emptiness within you. When dealing with this emptiness you will discover there is only a temporary relief through therapists, medication and seeing your offender in prison. For example, a girl who was a crown ward was sexually abused by her foster parent. When she became a young woman, she engaged in a lengthy court battle. She believed seeing her perpetrator found guilty for the sexual abuse she would be able to experience joy and contentment in life. While she made the right decision to pursue criminal charges, she believed she would feel better when he was found guilty. The perpetrator was found guilty and she did receive a sense of peace with the outcome of the criminal trial but a year later she found herself still feeling deep anger and resentment toward her abuser. She then commenced a lawsuit against her abuser and the organization responsible for her care. She was again successful with her lawsuit but a few months later she once more found herself discontent. She attended therapy for approximately 12 years but never addressed the actual impact of the abuse on her spiritual development. She remained unhappy and struggled to find joy in her life. Therapy did help her to establish healthy boundaries, assertive communication skills and positive self-talk however; therapy did not address the spiritual confusion. Unfortunately, her coping strategies left her feeling self-defeated and engaging in self-destructive behaviours.

Establishing coping skills that do not adequately address your spiritual development will only hinder you from experiencing contentment in life. While through no fault of your own, your underdeveloped spirituality could quite possibly cause you to become detached or misaligned in your relationship with God. To help you become more aligned with God and strengthen your relationship with Him, it is essential to understand and identify how your spiritual development became hindered. Perhaps it was in the area of participation or in the perception of church lifestyle, your religious beliefs or your understanding of salvation. Maybe you were lacking knowledge in the character of God, your intimacy with God, understanding your power to walk in God's ordained destiny for your life, or your inheritance as a daughter of the Most High God!

Spiritual Development
WORKSHEET

It is crucial for you to be able to identify the ways in which you have tried to cope with your abuse. Below is a list of the many ways in which your spiritual development may have been impacted by your abuse experiences. As an exercise, circle those items that you believe impacted your spiritual development.

CHURCH For those who are believers, church is understood in two ways. The church is a community of believers who confess Jesus Chris as Lord. Church also means people-a corporate identity of Christians. Scripture tells the body of believers to organize under qualified leadership. Therefore, church is a building, a place of worship.

- I see church as a safe place.

- I see church as unsafe place.

- I have a caring and compassionate leadership/pastor.

- I perceive church as patriarchal in practice, culture and oppressive toward women.

- I enjoy fellowship with other people at church.

- I have difficulty trusting clergy, pastors, and church leaders.

- I have healthy boundaries with people in authority such as church elders, pastors.

- I see people who attend church as hypocrites.

- I participate in a ministry area that allows me to use my gifting.

- I am too trusting of authority figures in the church.

- I seek to please authority figures in the church, instead of God.

- People are accepting of me and encourage me to grow spiritually. I am spiritually fed at church.

- I have to be perfect or get my life together before I can attend church.

SALVATION

Salvation is available in Jesus alone and is dependent on God alone for provision, assurance and security. Believing in Jesus Christ as the Son of God who died as the substitute for our sins is the only requirement for salvation. The Bible says that there is nothing we can do to earn our salvation. God, because of His grace, did all that needs to be done.

- I recognize that I do not have to earn my salvation.

- I misinterpret my suffering as a necessary condition for salvation.

- I have difficulty accepting the truth of God's word.

- I believe my salvation is secure.

- I have to work to earn my salvation and try to earn God's approval.

- I believe God accepts me as I am with all my faults and imperfections. I do not have to do anything to earn His love.

- I believe I need to be a perfect person before I can be saved.

- I believe Jesus is the son of God who died as a substitute for my sins, therefore this is the only requirement for my salvation.

CHARACTER OF GOD

The character of God is revealed through his son, Jesus. His character is shown through His covenant of love for you and all of creation. God is patience, sovereignty, holy, wisdom, faithful, just, righteous, kind, truth, and a promise keeper. God reveals His character to you in the Bible, teaching you through His words and from His interactions with people. Some aspects of His character are reserved just for Him. For example, He alone is omniscient, and He alone is self-sustaining. God is love that never changes.

- I merge the character of God with my abuser.

- I turn away from God; lost faith in God.

- I turn to God for comfort, guidance and love.

- I believe God is the full expression of love.

- I believe God's character is not defined by the behaviour and characteristics of my abuser.

- I struggle to see and believe in the true nature and character of God.

- I believe I am accepted and loved by God because of who I am.

- I am unable to recognize that I'm already approved and loved by God as I am.

- I see God as punitive and angry.

- I see God as the full and complete expression of love.

- I can't see God as God. (Luke 18:19)

- I see God as slow to anger.

- I see God as Lord of lords and King of kings.

- I see God as quick to anger and as a punisher. (Ps. 103:8, 1Tim. 1:16)

- I don't see God as Righteous and Just.

- I see God as righteous and just. (Deut. 32:4, 1saiah 45:19)

- I struggle to see God as All-Powerful. (Jeremiah 32:17, Psalm 8:3, Eph. 3:20, Philippians 4:13)

- I believe God is the full expression of love.

- I am unable to see God showing kindness toward those who don't deserve good. (Romans 3:23, 1 Peter 5:10)

- I believe God is all powerful and all knowing.

INTIMACY WITH GOD

Intimacy speaks of the degree of closeness in your relationship with God. God loves you and longs to have a close relationship with you. He wants you to have an intimate love relationship and friendship with Him. God desires you to spend time with Him and intimately communicate with Him, to enjoy fellowship with Him, to trust and follow Him, and to give your life meaning and purpose.

- I see God as present at all times and as involved in the affairs of my life.

- I don't see God as active and present in my life, situation or in the world.

- I believe God desires to have a personal and intimate relationship with me.

- I don't see God as personal and dwelling within me.

- I am able to receive God's love, grace and unmerited mercy.

- I have difficulty comprehending that God desires to have an intimate relationship with me.

- I have difficulty receiving God's love, grace and mercy.

- I feel guilt and shame because of the abuse and this contributes to my struggle to accept God's forgiveness and stops me from giving forgiveness to others.

- I acknowledge that God loved me first, even before I was created in my mother's womb.

- I reject God's demonstration of love toward me. (Romans 5:8)

- My fear keeps me in bondage and prevents me from seeing God as approachable, as my helper, protector, comforter and healer.

WALKING IN YOUR DESTINY

Destiny speaks of your purpose in life. God's sovereignty reaches you as a very specific plan for your life. Jeremiah 1:4-5 states God called the prophet, Jeremiah before he was even born. Psalm 139:16 shows that David also recognized that the Lord had a plan for his life. Samuel 23:9-12 indicates that this knowledge which David had, led him to seek the Lord for wisdom and guidance in many situations. God has a plan for your life which includes happiness in this world and eternity. Those who accept Christ as Savior have accepted God's plan for their life. Acceptance of God's plan is a daily commitment to follow God to allow him to order and guide you to fulfill your destiny.

- I am unable to see that God can use me for His glory.

- I am a willing vessel for the Lord. I recognize that God does not want me to be a martyr in my service to Him.

- I lack a desire to grow spiritually.

- I seek to know God's will for my life.

- I have difficulty honoring God and living a life that brings glory to Him. (1 Tim 1:17)

- Even though I make mistakes, I try my best to live a life that is pleasing to God. I believe God honors my efforts.

- I reject myself as a child of God.

- I believe God has an amazing plan for my life. I do not need to be educated or highly talented to be used by God. I recognize that God calls me to walk with excellence.

- I don't believe that God has a plan for me because I'm poor and/or uneducated.

CHILD OF GOD

God created all living things, so we are all his children. John 1:12 states to all who receive Christ, to those who believed in His name, He gave them the right to become children of God. 1 John 4:5 states when you have a relationship with God through Christ, you become a child of God.

- I go to God with all my struggles and problems.

- I love to worship God for who He is.

- I have counterfeit affections.

- I am unable to worship God in spirit and in truth. (John 4:24)

- I am unable to trust in His faithfulness. (Ps 100:5)

- I believe God will bless me. I am highly favored.

- I see God as faithful and never changing.

- I don't believe that God is able to bless me. (Numbers 6:23-27; 1Chron 4:10; 1 Peter 3:9)

Take a moment and reflect on the different areas in which your spiritual development may have been impacted by the abuse you have endured. Overall, has the abuse you experienced led you toward or away from God? Briefly explain.

_____

_____

_____

_____

_____

_____

_____

_____

_____

_____

_____

_____

_____

_____

CHAPTER TWO

You Are a Miracle Workbook: Treatment Modality

THE MAIN THERAPEUTIC APPROACH OF *YOU ARE A MIRACLE WORKBOOK* IS TRAUMA-FOCUSED COGNITIVE Behaviour Therapy. The Trauma Focused-Cognitive Behaviour Therapy model is used on clients' pre-existing faith to assist them in healing from the trauma of childhood sexual abuse. The therapeutic approach is only a tool to help guide you on your healing journey. Trauma-Focused Cognitive Behaviour Therapy is a type of psycho-educational treatment which helps you understand your thoughts and feelings as well as how they interact to influence your behaviour as a result of the trauma you've experienced. Trauma Focused-Cognitive Behaviour Therapy is an effective approach when working with survivors of childhood sexual abuse who were abused by a male or female perpetrator. According to McDonagh et al. (2005) this treatment modality is highly effective when working with women survivors of childhood sexual abuse. It has been empirically supported and has shown to successfully help survivors of childhood physical and sexual abuse (Cohen, Mannarino, Deblinger & Berlinger, 2009). This a treatment option that will empower you to manage your emotions, changes the way you think and creates positive behavioural changes which promote healing. Several research studies have shown that to victims of childhood abuse, religious and spiritual faith was profoundly damaged as a result of the abuse; whereas other survivors have attempted to make use of religious and spiritual resources to cope with and give meaning to the abuse (Walker, Reid, O'Neill, & Brown 2009). In treating childhood sexual abuse, Trauma Focused-Cognitive Behaviour Therapy is currently the leading treatment for recovery. Trauma Focused-Cognitive Behaviour Therapy focuses on an individual's pre-existing religious and spiritual functioning as well as changes in their religion and/or spirituality after abuse (Walker, Reese, Hughes & Troskie 2010). These researchers suggest that Trauma Focused-Cognitive Behaviour Therapy will assist clients from various religious/spiritual affiliations to process and recover from childhood sexual abuse (Walker et al, 2010).

Using your faith as a foundation, Trauma Focused-Cognitive Behaviour Therapy approach will teach you how to identify and change destructive, irrational and dysfunctional thoughts. The negative thoughts you hold will negatively impact your behaviour and your emotions. Trauma Focused-Cognitive Behaviour

Therapy approach will teach you how to modify your behaviour to promote emotional and psychological well-being. Survivors often experience thoughts or feelings that reinforce or compound faulty and ungodly beliefs. An erroneous belief system contributes to problematic behaviour that can affect various aspects of your life such as family, marriage, relationships, work, academics and your relationship with God. The faulty beliefs you hold will delay your healing journey or leave you stuck and unable to move forward. Consider this case example; a young woman who suffered the trauma of sexual abuse struggled to go to ask God to help her with her healing because she didn't understand why God did not prevent the abuse from occurring in the first place. She couldn't understand how he was all powerful and believed he did nothing to stop the abuse from continuing throughout her childhood. As she grew in her faith, she learned that God loved her and answers her prayers but she still couldn't feel his love and often struggled to receive his love. When she began to work through her painful experiences of abuse with the help of her pastor and a social worker, she learned more about how the effects of sexual abuse were interfering with her ability to experience joy in life. As she increased her understanding of Christ's atonement, applied God's word to her life, connected herself with fellow believers, she gained a better understanding of God's grace and mercy; finding comfort in prayer and spending time with God, addressing her barriers to forgiveness, increasing her understanding of the Gospel, learning strategies to manage strong symptoms, she was able to embrace God's love and find the peace and healing she longed for. Using God as the plumb line for her life, the pastor and social worker effectively integrated her faith with the trauma focused-cognitive behaviour therapy leading to healing in which this woman was able to find contentment and joy in her life.

There are three components of Trauma Focused-Cognitive Behaviour Therapy that interconnect creating a cycle:

1. Thought Restructuring

You Are A Miracle Workbook will help you to identify problematic thoughts and beliefs and help you change your destructive thoughts and behaviour. At this stage, you will spend a considerable amount of time examining, identifying and deconstructing the unhealthy thoughts that you hold. Work in this component will help you engage in an introspective process. This personal insight and self-discovery will help to reframe your thoughts as necessary for the treatment process to facilitate further healing.

At this stage, you will focus on how to change your current thoughts and beliefs. The cognitive reframing process will help you to replace your problematic, negative thought patterns with accurate, godly beliefs. This will reinforce and encourage you to see yourself the way God sees you. It will also help you to minimize spiritual conflicts and help you embrace a healthier identity in Christ and be more open to embrace the Father's love.

For example, a survivor of sexual abuse may think "I don't need anyone. I have lived much of my life feeling alienated and alone." As a result of this thought and actually believing it, she may continue to isolate herself and reject invitations to socialize with others. She ignores her hunger for closeness. Psalm 68:6 tells us that God sets the lonely in families. Embracing a God centered belief system; instead of thinking "I don't need anyone", a survivor may restructure her thought as "God has brought many people across my path. Some of those people remained for a short time, some remained for a long time, and some will remain for a lifetime. As a result of a God centered thought, she may stop ignoring her hunger for closeness and intimacy by accepting invites to social events. Overtime, she develops several healthy friendships.

2. Behaviour Modification

The second component of the Trauma Focus-Cognitive Behaviour Therapy process involves examining your specific behaviours (actions or inactions) that you are using to cope with the effects of sexual abuse. Once you are able to identify the behaviour that is helping you negatively cope, you will be taught how to implement new behaviour and skills to promote healing. Behaviour modification recognizes that behaviour can be a habit that will take time to change. I believe that all behaviour can be unlearned and replaced with healthier options; identifying behaviour that is maladaptive and then substituting it with adaptive behaviour will promote healing. Modifying your behaviour requires unlearning negative behaviour and substituting it with new behaviour. You will learn how to regulate your behaviour to help decrease stress, enhance your mood and reinforce positive beliefs in order to promote an improved sense of well-being and meaning in life. You work hard to change your behaviour by setting behaviour goals. You are then able to look at external and internal influences on your behaviour. This then empowers you to control your behaviour through self-regulation and self-reinforcement. You are also required to repeatedly practice your new behaviour until it becomes natural to you. *You Are A Miracle Workbook* will give you strategies to help you establish healthy behaviour patterns. For example, a depressed person may neglect socializing with friends. Behaviour modification strategy would encourage the depressed person to implement activities which help to increase his or her opportunities for socializing such as going out for coffee with a friend or attending a women's ministry event.

3. Emotions and Body Sensations

Another component of the Trauma Focused-Cognitive Behaviour Therapy approach requires you to understand, identify and release emotions. You may find it difficult to identify exactly how you are feeling. Psychological pain is also caused by negative thoughts and behaviour as the result of distressing, negative emotions or body sensations. Labeling body sensations as negative or a perceived threat will automatically influence the development of negative thoughts and behaviour; which can then increase or exacerbate difficult or uncomfortable body sensations.

The Trauma Focus-Cognitive Behaviour Therapy approach teaches that thoughts contribute to certain feelings. Experiencing negative/unwanted feelings or body sensations requires you to change your thoughts and behaviour to promote more desirable emotional reactions and/or minimize body sensations. You may be experiencing difficult emotions such as hopelessness, sadness, anger, shame, guilt or anxiety. You can however remain vulnerable to these negative emotions if you do not change how you think and how you behave. This approach will assist you in identifying and managing your overwhelming and difficult feelings/body sensations.

COGNITIVE BEHAVIOR THERAPY CYCLE

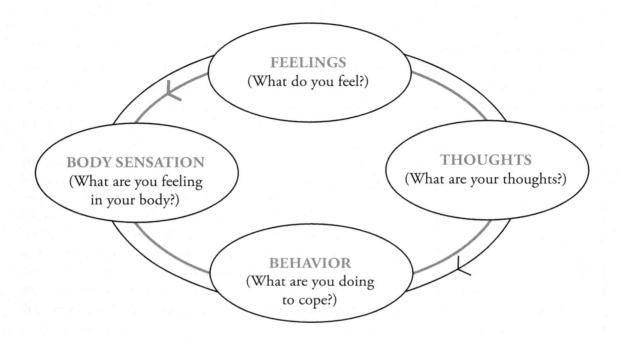

Basically, the interconnectedness of your feelings, thoughts and behaviour can create a cycle. The Trauma Focused-Cognitive Behaviour Therapy approach is more than just positive thinking. It examines the inter-relationship of your behaviour and thinking patterns to improve your mood and ultimately your spiritual growth and well-being.

For example, Sarah developed low self-esteem as a result of the sexual abuse she experienced as a child. She struggled throughout her life with feeling lonely. She suffered from hyper-arousal, feelings of fear and anxiety. She described herself as a "church hopper" and frequently stated "I don't attach to anybody." She found herself constantly running away from everyone, and the only place that she could find solace was to travel from church to church and remain disconnected from people. She made sure that she did not form relationships with people beyond hello and would only attend a given church for a few months, at most one year. Worshipping God at church gave her great peace and she loved going to church; however, she was scared that if people got to know her they would hate her. She feared rejection and tried to protect herself by failing to nurture relationships and keeping to herself. After 22 years of marriage, she and her husband divorced. She becomes depression over the following months. She felt little motivation to do daily activities. She felt tired, had difficulty concentrating and became increasing worried about her future.

Now using the above story about Sarah as an example, let's walk through the Cognitive Behaviour Therapy cycle to identify all 4 areas of the cycle to demonstrate a negative, ungodly belief expectation cycle.

FEELINGS: sadness, fear ++, hopeless

THOUGHTS: "No one will like me", "people will hate me if they get to really know me", "I need to protect myself so I don't attach/nurture relationships with others"

BODY SENSATIONS: heart rate acceleration, stomach sensations, sweaty palms

BEHAVIOUR: Sarah fails to foster or nurture relationships. She travels from place to place and does not establish roots at church

Sarah's belief expectation cycle does little to give her peace, meet her need for intimacy with others, give her a sense of belonging or acceptance and interferes with her having the opportunity to receive spiritual guidance, support and encouragement from the leadership and her church family. Here the inter-relationship of her thoughts and behaviour do little to reduce her fears, if anything it intensifies her fear to be close to people. Her beliefs about herself and the world were not balanced and were limited evidence to support her beliefs. Sarah was very selective in the evidence (information she believe to be fact). Having depression, she remembers only the rejection and hurt she experienced from her abuse which hinders her from forming relationships. Sarah focused on her abuser's treatment of her and ignored all the individuals in her life that are supportive and those who try to have friendship with her. Sarah concludes she is not an interesting person. Sarah may not even be aware that she formed a negative belief system. Such negative thoughts and beliefs keep her in a cycle of interaction with others that does not help her to heal, but rather keep her stuck in a vicious cycle.

Now let's take a look at the Sarah's situation using the Trauma Focused-Cognitive Behaviour Therapy model which incorporates her faith and acknowledges God's power operating with Sarah's faith. Sarah's more balanced cycle looks like this:

Thoughts: "God promises me, He will never leave me nor forsake me", "God will put people in my life that I will be a blessing to", "Others enjoy spending time with me."

Feelings: peace, acceptance, hopeful, less fear

Body Sensations: peace, no sweaty palms, normal heart rate and no stomach sensations

Behaviour: Sarah seeks the support of her pastor for spiritual care. The pastor meets with Sarah each month. After establishing a relationship with her pastor, she becomes more comfortable with connecting with other women in her church. Feeling safer and trusting people in the church, Sarah begins to attend social events at church and meets a woman with whom she develops an amazing friendship.

The balanced cycle promoted further healing just by changing Sarah's thoughts and behaviour while at the same time leading to improve her overall emotional functioning.

Using your existing faith as a foundation in Trauma Focused-Cognitive Behaviour Therapy model, will give you the tools to examine your belief system to make changes in the way that you think and behave to elevate your mood. A balanced or God-centered belief expectation cycle will reduce the intensity of difficult emotions; help you to change your self-talk to live life as your true authentic self!

CHAPTER THREE

Understanding Childhood Sexual Abuse

1. What is Childhood Sexual Abuse?

ACCORDING TO THE DEPARTMENT OF JUSTICE IN CANADA, CHILDHOOD SEXUAL ABUSE IS DEFINED AS THE sexual exploitation of a child by an adult. Sexual abuse may include one or more of the following:

• Being touched, fondled, looked at, spoken to, hugged and/or or kissed in a sexual way

• Oral and/or anal sex

• Rape and/or digital penetration

• Exposure to pornographic materials (including forced participation)

• Forced to watch adults engage in sexual behaviours

• Being forced to touch adults or yourself in a sexual way

2. What is Sexual Violence?

According to the Department of Justice in Canada, sexual violence includes many acts such as sexual assault, sexual harassment, rape, the murder of women, as well as other practices such as sexual exploitation and sexual slavery/prostitution. Sexual violence may involve one or more of the following factors:

• Forced oral, vaginal, and/or anal penetration

• Forced touching, kissing, and/or fondling

• Forced participation in sexual acts

• Forced sexual acts involving weapons or objects

- Forced exposure to sexual conduct

- Coerced sexual behaviour

- Forced exposure to sexual information

- Discrimination based on gender

- Sexual intimidation, threats and/or fear

3. Reasons why victims may not disclose sexual abuse in childhood:
There are many different reasons why victims may keep the abuse secret:

- *Age and/or developmental stage:* some children may be too young (developmentally, cognitively or emotionally) to clearly tell what is happening to them. They are too young to differentiate the behaviour as being wrong and inappropriate.

- *Feelings of powerlessness and hopelessness:* Some may feel trapped by circumstances or have been threatened that harm will come to them or someone close to them if they disclose the abuse.

- *Dependency:* They may be in a situation of dependency on the perpetrator.

- *Fear:* They may fear that no one will believe them. They may fear they will be stigmatized, and that their sexual identity will be called into question. They may be afraid of the perpetrator's reprisals or other negative consequences of telling others. They may want to protect family members (including the perpetrator).

- *Conflicting emotions:* They may feel confusion or shame. They may believe the abuse is their fault.

Even in cases where victims tell others about the abuse, the recipient may not report the abuse to authorities for reasons such as disbelief, shame, fear of and dependency on the perpetrator.

(Department of Justice Canada 2011-04-26)

4. The Impact of childhood sexual abuse on mental health:
According to Health Canada, the mental health effects include short-term and long-term consequences on children who were sexually abused. There are seven major psychological disturbances:

- Post traumatic stress disorder with immediate and long-term symptoms such as flashbacks, nightmares, and intrusive thoughts

- Cognitive distortions such as guilt, low self-esteem and self-blame

- Mood disorders such as depression and anxiety

- Dissociation which involves disengagement, detachment, numbing, and multiple personality disorders

- Relationship difficulties involving intimacy disturbances, altered sexuality, aggression, adversarial and manipulative behaviour

- Avoidance difficulties involving suicidal tendencies, self-mutilation and use of psychoactive substances

- Depression, stress symptoms, psychosomatic illness such as fatigue, insomnia, headaches, hostility, anger, distrust of others, competitiveness, spousal and child abuse and substance abuse

(Health Canada, 2011)

Other Consequences of Abuse:
Unhealthy dieting, poor communication style, promiscuity, sensitivity to criticism, dependency on others, social difficulties (withdrawn, loneliness), poor performance at work, low academic achievement, fixation with problems, not authentic

Statistics on Childhood
SEXUAL ABUSE

Police reported data for 2007 which indicated that female rates of sexual victimization were 5.6 times higher than male rates (120 versus 21 per 100,000 population). Brennan, Shannon & Taylor-Butts, Andrea (December 2008).

Females and youth were at particular risk of being sexually victimized. **Victimization and police-reported data both indicated that the rate of sexual victimization for females was about 5 times higher than the rate for males. Moreover, police-reported data indicated that over half of sexual assault victims in 2007 were children under the age of 18.** Brennan, Shannon & Taylor-Butts, Andrea (December 2008).

Children and youth under 18 years of age are at greatest risk of being sexually assaulted by someone they know. *Source: Family Violence in Canada: A Statistical Profile 2007. Canadian Centre for Justice Statistics. Catalogue No. 85-224-XIE, ISSN 1480-7165. Ottawa, Ontario, Canada. 2007. (Pg. 6, 21).*

Sexual assault against children by family members was more then three times higher for female victims than for male victims (108 compared with 32 incidents per 100,000 population). (Rates of sexual assault are higher for female victims than for male victims regardless of the relationship to the accused.) *Source: Family Violence in Canada: A Statistical Profile 2007. Canadian Centre for Justice Statistics. Catalogue No. 85-224-XIE, ISSN 1480-7165. Ottawa, Ontario, Canada. 2007. (Pg. 22).*

Parents represented 7 out of 10 family members accused of physical assault and 40% of those accused of sexual assault against children and youth. Statistics Canada, July 2005.

In 2005, girls under 18 years experienced rates of sexual assault that were almost four times higher than their male counterparts. (For every 100,000 young females there were 320 victims of sexual assault, compared to a rate of 86 male victims for every 100,000 young males.) *Source: Family Violence in Canada: A Statistical Profile 2007. Canadian Centre for Justice Statistics. Catalogue No. 85-224-XIE, ISSN 1480-7165. Ottawa, Ontario, Canada. 2007. (Pg. 21).*

In Canada in 2003, there were approximately 17, 321 child maltreatment investigations (3.64 investigations per 1,000 children) which involved allegations of sexual abuse during their childhood. Sexual abuse was substantiated in 23% of these investigations (3,958 investigations). An additional 16 % of sexual abuse cases were suspected but were not substantiated. Public Health Agency of Canada, Canadian Incident Study of Reported Child Abuse and Neglect-2003 Major Findings. (Pg. 39).

More than 90% of juvenile sexual abuse victims know their perpetrator in some way. Snyder, Howard, N. (2000, July). *Sexual assault of young children as reported to law enforcement: victim, incident, and offender characteristics.* Retrieved from http://bjs.ojp.usdoj.gov/content/pub/pdf/saycrle.pdf

Sexual assault against children by family members was more than three times higher for female victims than for male victims (108 compared with 32 incidents per 100,000 population). (Rates of sexual assault are higher for female victims than for male victims regardless of the relationship to the accused.) *Source: Family Violence in Canada: A Statistical Profile 2007. Canadian Centre for Justice Statistics. Catalogue No. 85-224-XIE, ISSN 1480-7165. Ottawa, Ontario, Canada. 2007. (Pg. 22).*

One in three girls and one in six boys experienced an unwanted sexual act. *Source: Child Sexual Abuse (The Canadian Badgley Royal Commission, Report on Sexual Offences Against Children and Youths), 1984. Pg. 175)*

These startling statistics demonstrate that sexual abuse is a societal problem and that you are not alone in your suffering. The statistics highlight that girls are more likely to be sexually abused or experience an unwanted sexual behaviour toward them by individuals they know personally or have direct contact with and are not necessarily strangers.

CHAPTER FOUR

Sexual Abuse In the Bible

WHAT DOES THE BIBLE SAY ABOUT SEXUAL VIOLENCE AND CHILD SEXUAL ABUSE? IN THE BIBLE, GOD SPEAKS the truth and reveals the tragic stories of sexual abuse, child abuse, rape, incest and family dysfunction. God forbids sexual abuse, incest and child abuse. God tells us about child abuse in Genesis 37:12-36, 1King 3:16-27, Isaiah 13:16, Ezekiel 9:6, Matthew 2:13-18, and Joel 3:3. While these verses speak of child abuse, they are not specific to sexual abuse. As you can see from these scriptures below, the spirit of lust sees no objectivity; only its own indulgence.

"So I say, live by the Spirit, and you will not gratify the desires of the sinful nature. For the sinful nature is contrary to the Spirit, and the Spirit is contrary to the sinful nature. They are in conflict with each other, so that you do not do what you want. But if you are led by the Spirit, you are not under the law." Galatians 5:16

"For everything in the world: the cravings of sinful man, the lust of his eyes and the boasting of what he has and does, comes not from the Father but from the world." 1 John 2:16

"Therefore do not let sin reign in your mortal body so that you obey its evil desires."
   Romans 6:12

Lust is a product of mankind's natural tendency to sin. Satan constantly appeals to a person's weakness. The bondage of lust causes people to engage in harmful thoughts and activities. In 2 Samuel 13: 1-3, Amnon, the son of David, fell into intense lust with Tamar, his half-sister, the beautiful sister of Absalom, son of David. As we read 2 Samuel 13:10-14 it says,

> "Then Amnon said to Tamar, "Bring the food here into my bedroom so I may eat from your hand." And Tamar took the bread she had prepared and brought it to her brother Amnon in his bedroom. But when she took it to him to eat, he grabbed her and said, "Come to bed with me, my sister." "Don't my brother!" she said to him. "Don't force me. Such

a thing should not be done in Israel! Don't do this wicked thing. What about me? Where could I get rid of my disgrace? And, what about you? You would be like one of the wicked fools in Israel. Please speak to the king; he will not keep me from being married to you." But he refused to listen to her, and since he was stronger than she, he raped her."

After sexually assaulting his sister, Amnon violently rejects her. Amnon says to her, "Get up and get out!" We later learn that in her emotional distress and rejection, weeping loudly, Tamar puts ashes on her head and tore the ornamented robe she was wearing. Her brother Absalom said to her, "Has that Amnon, your brother, been with you? Be quiet now, my sister; he is your brother. Don't take this thing to heart." And Tamar lived in her brother Absalom's house, a desolate woman. When King David heard that Tamar was sexually abused, he was furious, but did nothing. At verse 19 to 22, Absalom never said a word to Amnon, neither good nor bad; he hated Amnon because he had disgraced his sister Tamar. Tamar spoke out against the rape but had her voice silenced by her brother, Absalom, who desired to hide the family secret. It appears that King David and Absalom disapproved of Amnon raping Tamar, yet they did very little to show their support and this contributed to her remaining a desolate woman. Tamar needed an earthly father who took steps to protect, affirm and validate her, but her father ignored her and enabled the abuse.

Sexual abuse has been a tool Satan has used to wage war on God's children. Satan uses childhood sexual abuse in an attempt to destroy you and your identity by damaging your natural childlike responsiveness to turn toward God, your Father and your ability to trust in His love. As we look closer at Tamar's experiences, you may wonder if God even gets involved in this situation. We learn later in the Bible, God imposed the death penalty on the perpetrator.

In the Bible, God also tells us women should be treated with honor. Deuteronomy 22:25-26 states, "But if out in the country a man happens to meet a young girl pledged to be married and rapes her, only the man who has done this shall die. Do nothing to the girl; she has committed no sin deserving death." We can see in this scripture that God does not condone the rape and punishes the rapist. **God loves his daughters including you**. You are His greatest joy and He created you with an inherent worth. Matthew 18:6 reads, "But if anyone causes one of these little ones who believe in me to sin, it would be better for him to have a large millstone hung around his neck and to be drowned in the depths of the sea." Here Jesus is saying this form of punishment would be more an act of mercy compared to what would befall a person who has caused his daughter to turn from Christ's way. Jesus is giving a strong warning to people against causing his daughters to lose their faith in Him. God is not telling you to take things into your own hands but He himself will avenge you, His precious daughter.

Isaiah 61: 1-3, scripture states:

> The Spirit of the Sovereign LORD is on me, because the LORD has anointed me to preach good news to the poor. He has sent me to bind up the brokenhearted, to proclaim freedom for the captives and release

from darkness for the prisoners, to proclaim the year of the LORD's favor and the day of vengeance of our God, to comfort all who mourn, and provide for those who grieve in Zion—to bestow on them a crown of beauty instead of ashes, the oil of gladness instead of mourning, and a garment of praise instead of a spirit of despair. They will be called oaks of righteousness, a planting of the LORD for the display of his splendor.

Is the Lord speaking of his daughters who were sexually violated? Absolutely! This scripture speaks to His daughters who have experienced sexual abuse and/or violence, who are poor in heart. His daughters are the captives who are in bondage, captive to sin and need to be freed from the natural negative outcomes of sexual abuse. The effects of childhood sexual abuse on you can include post-traumatic stress disorder, anxiety and depression, propensity to further victimization in adulthood, physical injury to the child and long term psychological trauma. Sexual abuse may lead you to have difficulties in social, sexual and interpersonal functioning and can interrupt your spiritual development. The fundamental damage caused by the trauma of sexual abuse can hinder your developing capacity for trust, intimacy, autonomy and sexuality and mental health problems in adulthood. You may be imprisoned in your ungodly beliefs or certain ways of thinking because of the sexual violence. However, Christ alone is able to unlock those strongholds in your mind, reverse the effects of sexual abuse on your life and set you free from all the damaged caused by the trauma of abuse! Jesus is willing to comfort you in your suffering with His assurance that He is able to turn your sadness into Joy! He is able to turn your complaints into the songs of praise! God works to make you more like Christ. He is the source of your righteousness. God is able to transform you into a woman who walks in victory, no longer weak and defeated. He alone is able to change your life by interrupting the laws of nature making you a Miracle!

A miracle is described as an event that occurs as a result of divine intervention. A miracle is often thought of as a perceptible interruption of the laws of nature. The law of nature theory implies that because of childhood sexual abuse, survivors are destined to be damaged in many ways such as mental health problems, psychological trauma and so forth. However, God alone is able to interrupt this natural course of action by working with the laws of nature to perform miracles. God's divine providence also allows him to work against the laws of nature to perform miracles in the lives of childhood sexual abuse survivors. For example, a little girl grows up in a horrendous home of domestic violence, poverty and endured years of sexual abuse at the hands of her father from the age of five to eighteen. She accepts Christ as her personal savior and Lord as a young adult. As a Christian she develops her faith and increasingly trusts God to improve her life. She surrenders her life daily to God and asks him to make her more like the woman he created her to be. Totally dependent on God, she later earns three university degrees, has a strong marriage, has strong relationships with her children and is financially secure. She looks back over her life and sees God's handiwork through every challenge in her life. She is able to testify that God intervened in her life making her a miracle!

ACTIVITY

Let's examine the scripture Isaiah 61:1-3. Read the scripture again and fill in the blanks below. What does God promise His daughters who have endured sexual abuse?

and provide for those who grieve in Zion—to bestow on them _____ instead of ashes, _____ instead of mourning, and a _____ instead of a spirit of despair. They will be called _____, a planting of the LORD for the display of his splendor.

MODULE TWO
Cognition

Understanding Your Thinking

CHAPTER FIVE

Benevolent or Punishing God

Do you see God as benevolent or punishing? How you perceive God and your relationship with Him can promote or delay your healing. Having a perception of God that mirrors your relationship with the abuser can make healing from sexual abuse complex, but not impossible. Researchers suggest that your perception of God reflects your relationship with your parental figures (Ganje-Fling & McCarthy 1996). If you experienced negative parental relationships, then you may experience a similar negative attachment and perception of God. A female survivor of childhood sexual abuse may perceive God, her heavenly father, as an abuser, just like her earthly father or the male figure who abused her (Kennedy 2003). This can lead to difficulties praying, having faith and trusting in a "male" God. If you view God as punishing, wrathful, distant and conditional, you may also have low self-esteem and perceive yourself unworthy of love, guilty of wrongdoings and deserving of punishment (Lemoncelli and Carey 1996). Therefore, how you perceive God correlates with how you perceive yourself.

Just as childhood sexual abuse can have a negative effect on how you view God, it can also affect the level of intimacy in your relationship with God, as well as your spiritual and psychological functioning, other relationships, and your overall well-being (Gall et al 2009). This negative image of God can contribute to your confusion about values, beliefs and thoughts if you believe that God is punishing you for your sins. An image of God as being cruel, uncaring, powerless and punishing may occur because of the abuse and can lead to lower levels of spiritual well-being, damaging your relationship with God and contributing to a reduced or over involvement in religious practice. It is possible that you may feel less loved and accepted by God because of the abuse. Feelings of guilt and shame may leave you feeling disconnected or rejected by God. You may feel intense anger toward God and distrust Him and one's religion, especially if you have been abused by someone in the church or a church leader.

On the other hand, many women who have experienced sexual abuse in their childhood can develop a positive outlook on life and still maintain a strong relationship with God. An image of a benevolent God instead of a punishing, wrathful God can lead to incredible healing! This means seeing God as always kind, friendly, willing to help, caring, generous, gracious, unselfish, charitable, supportive, helpful and desiring to do good not evil. Having a positive view of God increases the likelihood that you will use healthy coping strategies and develop a strong sense of self-worth. Your relationship with a benevolent God operates on many levels, especially on a cognitive level to provide you with an orienting framework for understanding and responding to the impact of sexual abuse and other stressful life events (Dull & Skokan 1995; Paragament 1997).

Researchers, Post & Wade (2009) tell us those survivors who believed they had a loving God to turn to for support resulted in them having less negative moods, depression and provided a greater sense of personal growth, hope, self-acceptance and resolution of the abuse. In addition, Hall (1995) found that individuals with a history of childhood sexual abuse who perceived God as a caring God resulted in improving their life in different areas, and women were more likely to participate in out-patient instead of in-patient treatment programs. Many survivors had a sense of life purpose, which appeared instrumental in overcoming the abuse and maintaining a sense of well-being in adulthood (Post & Wade, 2009). Survivors were able to develop the ability to secure social support, have a sense of positive self-regard, external attribution of blame for the abuse, perceive internal control and increase their sense of spirituality and intimacy in their relationship with God. Post & Wade (2009) found survivors whose belief in a benevolent God helped to protect them against the development of depression, shame and interpersonal difficulties.

Survivors were able to experience support in their relationships with God, church, and religion, which helped them to heal from the effects of childhood sexual abuse (Glaister & Abel 2001). Survivors were able to see God as a source of refuge in crisis that provided a secure base for exploring and making meaning of life events (Rowatt & Kirkpatrick, 2002). Survivors who accepted a benevolent God were able to see God as a constant source on which they could rely on for a sense of personal safety and emotional comfort (Post & Wade, 2009). Their relationship with a benevolent God gave them higher levels of hope, self-acceptance, more personal growth, and a greater sense of resolution of the abuse. They also had better interpersonal relationships and general coping skills in adult life (Paragament, 1997). Survivors who trust in a benevolent God and perceive God as having some control over their life were able to accept and understand their abuse experiences. In addition, Post & Wade (2009) tell us survivors were able to accept their personal limitations without self-denigration and see their lives as part of a greater purpose. Seeing their lives as part of a greater purpose helped them to heal from their abuse.

Individuals with a history of childhood sexual abuse who believe in a loving God are able to see God's handiwork and fingerprint in their situation. These survivors are less likely to think that God criticizes and punishes them. They tend to see God mainly as a force of positive influence on their lives and the world, and who is less likely to condemn them. Women who believe God loves them feel free to call on Him to answer their prayers in their time of need and see Him as their healer and comforter. Two women with different images of God, interpret God's actions and motivations differently in the same situation. A woman with a negative view of God is more likely to believe that God caused her abuse to happen, allowed it to happen to teach her a lesson or because He does not love her. A woman with a loving image of God is unlikely to blame God for causing the abuse. Rather, evidence of God's presence is found in her story of amazing miracles that saved her in the midst of her situation. She is able to see there is no favor too great for Him to give her. She does not think she is too insignificant for God to bless. She believes God is ever ready to give the greatest blessings to her, whatever her condition. She believes that God comes close to her side and takes every opportunity to do good for her. She sees Him as loving and caring. A survivor's perception of God directly influences her healing journey.

How do you perceive god? Do you view God as a benevolent heavenly father? Why or why not?

_____

_____

_____

_____

_____

_____

_____

_____

_____

_____

Do you perceive God as wrathful, cruel, powerless and uncaring? Why or Why not?

_____

_____

_____

_____

_____

_____

_____

_____

_____

_____

What factors (people or events) have influenced your perception of God? Explain briefly.

_____

_____

_____

_____

_____

_____

_____

_____

YOU ARE A MIRACLE

Do you see the fingerprint of God in your life? Please take a moment and write down where and how you see God working in your life. If you don't see where He is working in your life, ask God to reveal Himself to you.

_____

_____

_____

_____

_____

_____

_____

_____

_____

_____

_____

_____

_____

_____

_____

_____

_____

_____

_____

_____

_____

_____

_____

_____

CHAPTER SIX

A Benevolent God Who Heals

How does having a relationship with a benevolent God promote healing? While there are different spiritual models and theories on how a woman's relationship with God helps her heal from childhood sexual abuse or sexual violence, most of these models fail to take into account the power of Jesus to touch and transform her life! These models present God as a passive participant that is influenced by others. *You Are a Miracle Workbook* suggests that the relationship with a benevolent God has a *direct* impact on transforming your life, causing a dramatic reduction in your negative mood, a greater sense of personal spiritual growth, healing and restoration of your relationships. *You Are A Miracle Workbook* acknowledges that God alone transforms you. The depth and degree of healing depends on your readiness for change and willingness to release your struggles to God, giving him permission to heal the different areas in your life. To illustrate the model, consider a prism. The light refracted through a prism causes a rainbow to occur. When light passes through the prism, the different colors bend at different angles and then separate to produce the rainbow of light. God unconditionally loves each of His daughters in ways that cause different degrees of transformation and different results.

The spectrum of change is different for each woman because her experiences, makeup and needs are unique. The types of abuse and the impact of the abuse is different for each woman, therefore, the spectrum of change will be unique to you. God knows what you need and carefully attends to each need to heal you in whatever area in your life you desire change. Do you want to be less angry? Do you want to be able to say NO and not feel guilty? Do you want to restore relationships? What aspect or area in your life do you want God to transform?

God in His infinite power is able to preserve your life and guide your steps. He alone restores the survivor. Since God is all-powerful and all-wise, He has the ability and strength to bring to pass whatsoever He desires and the power to bring something into being. In Isaiah 46:10 God says, "I make known the end from the beginning, from ancient times, what is still to come. I say: My purpose will stand and I will do all that I please." There is no abuse too strong that Jesus cannot heal. God has made the earth though

His power. Jeremiah 32:17, it says "Ah, Sovereign Lord, you have made the heavens and the earth by your great power and outstretched arm. Nothing is too hard for you." God alone is able to heal and deliver you from the consequences of the sexual abuse you experienced.

WITHOUT GOD'S LOVE
NO PERSONAL TRANSFORMATION

**ANGER
LOW SELF-ESTEEM
DEPRESSION
ANXIETY
FEAR
BROKEN RELATIONSHIP
INSECURITY**

WITH GOD'S LOVE
HEALING FROM SEXUAL ABUSE

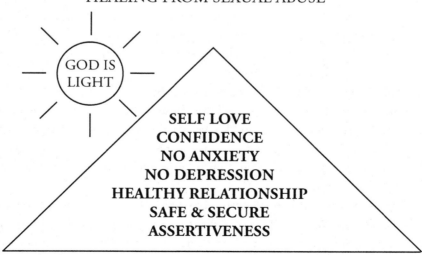

GOD IS LIGHT

**SELF LOVE
CONFIDENCE
NO ANXIETY
NO DEPRESSION
HEALTHY RELATIONSHIP
SAFE & SECURE
ASSERTIVENESS**

You Are A Miracle Workbook acknowledges that although God has the ultimate power to restore you, He will not force His power on you. *You Are a Miracle Workbook* recognizes that there is a collaborative & progressive relationship between you and God. The collaborative process happens when you **surrender to God** and **let Him change your life**! You access God as the source to help you in your healing journey. This collaborative and progressive relationship requires your response by becoming an active participant in the healing process. God has given you freewill to make the decision to enter into a relationship with Him and allow Him to transform your life with His love. Freewill allows you to make choices. Your freedom to make choices does not alter or lessen God's existence, knowledge or power. God knows in advance what choices you will make. He does not alter your natural ability to make choices. You have the ability to evaluate your options: to resist God or be open to His healing power. God's unconditional love for you is that He gave you the capacity and freedom to do what you want. God's unconditional love for you gives you the choice to follow him, allowing Him to restore your life or reject what He has to offer. *You Are A Miracle Workbook* acknowledges that God knows everything that happened to you and what will happen to you in the future. Psalm 139:2-6 declares God's knowledge about you. Psalm 139:2-6 states, "you know when I sit and when I rise; you perceive my thoughts from afar. You discern my going out and my lying down; you are familiar with all my ways. Before a word is on my tongue you know it completely, O Lord. You hem me in—behind and before; you have laid your hand upon me. Such knowledge is too wonderful for me, too lofty for me to attain." This scripture exemplifies to us that God is concerned with everything about you, including the abuse you experienced that was not your choice.

2 Corinthians 1:8b-9 states, that "We were under great pressure, far beyond our ability to endure, so that we despaired even of life. Indeed, in our hearts we felt the sentence of death. But this happened so that we might not rely on ourselves but on God, who raises the dead." Do you want to rely on God to help you heal from the consequences of your abuse? It's never too late to choose to heal. It's never too late to fall in love with the beautiful person God created you to be. Making the choice to allow God to heal your life is to reclaim your innocence...something that no one can take from you. *You Are A Miracle Workbook* emphasizes the power of God to transform, but ultimately it is up to you to make the choice to allow God into your life to help you heal. Essentially, your healing journey becomes a conscious choice in which you respond to the power of God so He can shine His light into your darkness. Do you want to be an active participant in your healing journey? God wants to transmit and impart divine qualities and attributes into the core of your personality. Operating from the place of grace, God lavishes his love, joy and peace on you, transforming the various areas in your life that require restoration and healing.

Wholeness with God

This program you have been following so far has been prepared to free you from your past; the act(s) of others against you, the shame, false guilt, memory difficulties from which God and I mean for you to be free. This was not sin you committed but was sin committed by another against you, yet you still need and long to be free. By God's grace you will be! In order to be completely free and whole you need to also be free from the guilt that is your own responsibility; the wrong **you** have done (lies, anger, gossip, etc.) as opposed to what others may have done to you. These things the Bible calls sin and are ultimately acts by you against God. We are all in the same boat. The Bible says that "all have sinned". The trouble is that sin separates us from a Holy God who made us to have fellowship with Him. When this fellowship is broken by sin we are not whole in our spirit. But we can be. We can be whole within. We can be reconciled to God in fact His Spirit can and will reside in you to restore you. Do you want to be reconciled to God?

If you have not made the decision and you are ready to become a Christian, ready to have a relationship with God, then say this prayer. You can say it using your own words as this prayer is only a guide.

A PRAYER OF SALVATION:

"Dear God, I come before you in the name of Jesus. I acknowledge that I am a sinner and ask for your forgiveness of my sins. Lord, I believe your son, Jesus, died on the cross to save me from my sins and He rose again from the dead. Jesus, thank you for dying on the cross for me! Lord, some of my sin was an outcome of the abuse I experienced and other sin was from choices that I made. I repent of my sins (intentional and unintentional). I want to open my heart to your love and live a life that is pleasing to you. I pray and ask Jesus to be my personal Savior and Lord over my life. Lord, fill me with your Holy Spirit. Lord, thank you for forgiving me of my sins and giving me eternal life! In Jesus' name I pray. Amen."

If you have prayed this prayer and believe it, you have been born again! I want to welcome you into God's family! God will be your constant companion from this day forward! Be blessed and I pray the Lord will continue to transform your life - YOU ARE A MIRACLE!

If you did not accept the invitation to become a Christian that's absolutely okay. Continue to use this book as it will increase your faith and provide you with valuable strategies to help you on your healing journey. Be blessed and I pray the Lord will continue to transform your life - YOU ARE A MIRACLE!

CHAPTER**SEVEN**

The Promises of God

"Our God is in control so we can have hope in the midst of the chaos of
this world. It doesn't matter what our circumstances are - good or bad.
We can always find joy with the Lord."

Rev. E. Mutale

GOD DID NOT WANT THE ABUSE TO HAPPEN TO YOU! MANY WOMEN WHO EXPERIENCE CHILDHOOD SEXUAL abuse, try to gain an understanding of their experiences by asking God many questions. These questions are laden with spiritual confusion and various emotions. These emotions are normal and appropriate for your spiritual, psychological and emotional healing. Sometimes women ask God questions such as:

"Lord, why did you let this happen to me?"
"Lord if you are so powerful why did you permit these things to happen?"
"Lord, don't you love me?"
"Do you even care about me?"
"How is this God's goodness toward me?"
"Do you really exist?"
"Who am I?"

We have absolutely permission to ask these questions of God, but it's more important that you learn to *listen for God's answers. (See chapter 13 strategies to help you to listen better to God's voice).* Have you been listening to God's answers to your questions? The scripture tells us that because of the original sin through Adam and Eve, we were separated from God. The original sin affects everyone born since then, so sin affects every generation including innocent children. What you experienced was not because you deserved it or because God wanted it to happen to you, it was the impact of the original sin. To illustrate, visualize what it's like when you take a rock and skip it across the water. Each ripple influences the next ripple and so on. It makes several ripples on the water before it rests. God desires to meet you at that resting place.

God is angry that the abuse happened to you. Luke 17:1-2 says, "If anyone causes one of these little ones who believe in me to sin, it would be better for him to be thrown into the sea with a large millstone tied around his neck." This scripture tells us that it's not acceptable to harm someone, but instead highlights God's view about harming His innocent children, including you. Your Heavenly Father knows you intimately and He desires to be your helper, protector and comforter. 1 Corinthians 10:13 states, "No temptation has seized you except what is common to man. And God is faithful; He will not let you be tempted beyond what you can bear." There are moments in life when you may feel that no one understands what you are going through. At times you may feel that you are not able to make it through, because of what you have to endure. God is telling you that although it feels unbearable, you will get through it! He also reassures you that he will not give you more than you can withstand. He knows the strength you have within you and will show you with His grace what you can stand against. When you are tempted with a difficult circumstance, He will also provide a way so you can stand up under it. During difficult times like these you must cling to His promises, knowing that no matter how hopeless your circumstances might be, you are not alone. He will certainly stand with you and see you through!

There is no scripture in the Bible that tells us that Jesus promises to spare you from suffering. Let's take a look at this poem; it highlights God's promises to you.

GOD'S PROMISE
God didn't promise
days without pain,
laughter without sorrow
or sun without rain.
But God did promise
strength for the day,
Comfort for the tears
And a light for the way.
And for all who believe
in His kingdom above,
He answers their faith
With everlasting love.
Author Unknown

God promises to be with you, constantly present in your storms. He wants to get your attention and wants every obstacle out of the way that stops Him from being in your life. God will provide you with a way to escape from the effects of the abuse when you take steps of faith. He knows you also have the ability and the strength within you to overcome the effects of abuse if you let Him heal you. The impact of the abuse may cause you to run from God's presence and from His will for your life. In the midst of your

36

circumstances you will discover areas of your character that need to be developed! As you ask God to help you with your struggles, His constant presence in your life will allow you to witness His power which will strengthen and transform you.

It is easy to have a positive attitude when times are going good, but when you are trying to overcome the impact of past abuse, it can be very difficult at times to have a positive attitude and victorious mindset. Scripture challenges you not to give in to a negative mindset, but encourages you to trust God. In the book of Job, God allowed Satan to do many things to Job except kill him. When we study Job's reaction, he says, "Though He slay me, yet will I hope in Him; I will surely defend my ways to His face." Despite his difficulties, Job remains hopeful that God will intervene in his situation. Job 1:21 Job states, "The Lord gave and the Lord has taken away, may the name of the Lord be praised." We learn that Job does not understand why God has permitted the things to occur to him, but he knew God is good so he continued to trust in Him. Job's attitude toward his situation gives us an indication to how we should be. James 1:2-4 reads, "Consider it pure joy, [my sister] when you face trials of many kinds, because you know that the testing of your faith develops perseverance. Perseverance must finish its work so that you may be mature and complete, not lacking anything. God will give you the strength to persevere.

This scripture challenges you to think differently about the entire experience of abuse and the healing process. Trials are an opportunity to mature in your faith and character, revealing whether your walk with God is genuine. Life is full of trials because we live in a troubled, fallen world. Challenges are an opportunity to test and destroy false or superficial faith. Trials cause a purifying and developing faith that is authentic. Yes, sometimes bad things happen to good people who seem undeserving of them. However, you must remember that God is good, just, loving and merciful. Often things happen to you that you simply cannot understand. Instead of doubting God's goodness, I would encourage you to trust Him. Trust in the LORD with all your heart and lean not on your own understanding; in all your ways acknowledge Him, and He will make your paths straight (Proverbs 3:5-6).

What is your attitude toward your abuse?

_____

_____

_____

_____

_____

_____

Do you desire God to heal you? What do you think might be getting in the way?

_____

_____

_____

_____

From 2 Kings 2:21 we learn God used Elisha to heal the water. The water in Jericho was not good for drinking or watering crops, preventing the fruit on the trees to ripen. People can't live without clean water, so the men of Jericho went to Elisha, a man of God, to ask for help. A miracle was necessary to improve the quality of the water. Then Elisha went out to the spring and threw salt into it, saying, "This is what the Lord says; I have healed this water. Never again will it cause death or make the land unproductive." God used the salt to provide the people with living water. Curing the water was symbolic of God's grace, preservation and purification.

If God could put salt on three things that need to be changed in your life, what would they be? List the areas.

1. _____

2. _____

3. _____

Here is a sample healing prayer that you may pray at this time. You may wish to personalize it to fit your situation.

> *"Lord, I ask you to put salt on (list the three items above) that was caused by the sexual abuse I experienced. I ask that you put the cross between me and (the three items listed above). Lord, I ask you to heal my spirit and my soul that was damaged in any way. Lord, I thank you that you are my healer. I pray for all the consequences of the abuse I experienced to be healed, that all fear and panic attacks stop, that nightmares cease, and that the memory of my experiences be healed in the name of Jesus. I love you and thank you that you are healing me. Thank you for providing me with daily strength. Thank you for loving me as I am. Thank you for your continued presence in my life. In Jesus' name I pray. AMEN."*

CHAPTER EIGHT

Ungodly Beliefs

Your belief system influences the decisions you make, your attitude toward yourself and others, your judgments, your expectations, which also impacts how you orientate yourself in the world. Ungodly beliefs are negative beliefs that you may hold that do not agree with God's truth, God's Word or God's character. Your ungodly beliefs are established and rooted in your sinful nature as a human being, your family and cultural beliefs and most likely from your traumatic experience. Many of these ungodly beliefs are established from the sexual abuse you experienced as a child. They have their roots in your early childhood when your spirit is most receptive and sensitive. These unhealthy beliefs that were established in early childhood are still affecting you today!

Ungodly beliefs are the lies you believe about yourself, other people and about God. Your ungodly beliefs affect who you are, how you perceive yourself and others, how you interact with others and your relationship with God. Essentially, what you believe in your heart to be true is how you behave and live out your life. In Proverbs 23:7a it reads, "As a man thinks in his heart, so is he." This scripture states you are a product of your thinking; you become what you think! Unhealthy beliefs that you hold give Satan permission to operate in your life. Satan will do everything he can to keep you trapped in this unhealthy mindset which hinders you from walking in your destiny and prevents you from living the abundant life God promised and desires for you! Ungodly beliefs also include thoughts that dishonor parents and authorities, condemning judgments, negative expectations, and negative words spoken over you or by you.

Ungodly beliefs appear to be absolutely true and seem to be based on perceived facts, yet based on God's Word, they are absolutely FALSE. Ungodly beliefs, not in line with God's truth about you, are intensified by your mistaken beliefs or wrong thinking pattern. The danger with ungodly beliefs is once they are ingrained into your spirit or hidden in your heart, you may not realize that you are living your life patterned after them. For instance, as a survivor of childhood sexual abuse, like most survivors, you may have a high need for control due to the loss of power and control that a victim of sexual abuse experiences.

As a result of the abuse, your ungodly belief may be---*I need to make sure I don't get hurt again!* This negative belief then may manifest as you having a desire to control situations and interactions with others. In your efforts to maintain control when interacting with others, you may find yourself being stubborn and/or rigid, have frequent power struggles, be passive aggressive, establish co-dependent relationships or conform to the wishes of others (*We will discuss co-dependent relationships in chapter 19, Godly Relationships*). All of these ways of interacting with others is a way to protect yourself from feeling vulnerable. However, this belief will strongly contribute to you having negative outcomes and reinforcing your initial ungodly belief.

BELIEF EXPECTATION CYCLE

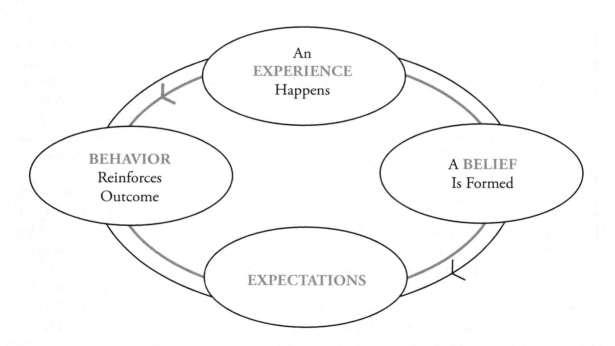

Ungodly beliefs are developed when you take the perceived facts of a situation, experience or event and label the facts as the truth about yourself. Once you have come into agreement with the ungodly belief, it will form certain expectations of others, yourself or God called a belief-expectation cycle. These expectations affect your behaviour, which will also cause you to influence the behaviour of others. This leads to more painful experiences, which will reinforce your ungodly belief and leave you trapped in a vicious negative cycle. Basically, your expectations can become self-fulfilling prophecies that reinforce your negative beliefs. Your ungodly belief system hinders your ability to grow in your faith in God and trust in His promises for your life. Ungodly beliefs also prevent God from blessing you because you are more likely to rely on yourself and not depend on Him. They prevent you from having healthy relationships, keep you overly sensitive to what others think of you, instead of how God actually sees you. They justify the ways of the flesh, hinder you from having a victorious mindset and lead you to behave in ways that cause you and others to sin. Ungodly beliefs undermine and disrupt your relationship with God and keep you in fear, which prevents you from fulfilling the plan or destiny God has for your life.

If you have developed a negative belief-expectation cycle it is possible to break it and create a more positive, healthy cycle. You can change your belief-expectation cycle. Your perception of the situation may clearly support your ungodly belief, thus causing you to resist adopting a new, godly belief system. To change your ungodly beliefs, you must first recognize that you believe something that is ungodly or false, which does not line up with God's truth about you. Then, you have to choose to believe something that is godly instead. It is important when dealing with ungodly beliefs to have a corresponding godly belief that is *meaningful to you* and does not simply contradict the ungodly belief. You also need to practice applying the new belief in your life. Satan will try to distract you to maintain that ungodly belief. Your newly acquired Godly beliefs will be challenged by things that may happen. In those moments, when your godly belief is being challenged, you have the choice of thinking of the way that is familiar to you, or thinking in accordance with your new godly beliefs.

HOW TO IDENTIFY UNGODLY BELIEFS

Take a moment to see if you are able to identify one or two lies (ungodly beliefs) that you want to change. If you can't come up with one, ask yourself the following question:

In what area of my life am I not achieving success or reaching my goals? In the space below, write down all the thoughts you have about this area in which you perceive as unsuccessful, no matter how silly or insignificant the thought.

_____

_____

_____

_____

_____

_____

IDENTIFYING UNGODLY BELIEFS

Now ask yourself the following questions:

1. Does my belief empower me? (If it doesn't empower you, then it is probably an ungodly belief.)

2. Does the belief promote a negative mood or positive mood? (If it does not make you feel better then it is probably an ungodly belief.)

3. Does this belief motivate me to do more or less? (If it makes you want to give up or feel hopeless then it is probably an ungodly belief.)

4. Does the belief encourage me to engage in self-destructive behaviour such as self-mutilation, addictions, and/or promiscuity? (If it promotes self-destructive behaviour, then it is probably an ungodly belief.)

5. Do I feel this belief limits my choices? (If it makes you feel restricted and you believe you have no alternatives, then it's probably an ungodly belief.)

6. When in my life was this belief not true for me? (If it seems like it's always true of you, then it's probably an ungodly belief.)

7. What is the purpose of this belief? (If the purpose keeps you trapped in fear or from achieving success, then it is probably an ungodly belief.)

Here are some statements that will help you identify ungodly beliefs. Put a cross beside each ungodly belief that you have.

- I should stay away from people because they will abandon me.

- I cannot trust people because they will always hurt me.

- I cannot relate to people. I don't have friends.

- I can't handle change.

- I will always be angry with myself, others and God.

- I will always be alone because I don't belong.

- I will always question people's motives because people think the worst of me.

• I have to hide my body because I am unattractive.

• I must control things around me to feel safe and to avoid being hurt again.

• I will always be_____ (depressed, angry, insecure).

• I will always have_____ (chaos, financial problems, relationship problems).

• God favors other people more than He loves me.

• I don't have any spiritual gifts.

• God does not always fulfill His promises.

• I have to earn people's acceptance by_____.

• I will never experience JOY.

• I judge and dishonor_____ (myself, parents, authority figures, siblings).

• I have missed opportunities to improve my life, so there is no point trying.

• I will never be able to receive love or give love to others.

• No one appreciates me.

• I will always be a failure.

• People will always reject me.

• People will only love me if _____.

• What I do in secret is okay.

• I will always be addicted to _____ (food, drugs, alcohol, shopping).

• No one likes who I am, so I need to be someone else. No one likes the real me.

• Bad things always happen to me.

• Taking steps to heal is too painful. I can't handle my emotions.

• People will always use and abuse me.

How many of the above statements did you put a cross beside? Do these statements agree with God's Word? You are right! The statements do not agree with God's truth and they are NOT true of you!

CHAPTER NINE

You Are the Goodness of God

YOU ARE AN IMAGE OF GOD'S GOODNESS AND GLORY! HAVE YOU STOPPED DREAMING OR DO YOU STRUGGLE to find joy in your life? The trauma of sexual abuse can impact all aspects of your life. One of the most common things that survivors experience is a change in how they perceive themselves and the world around them. You may automatically begin to define yourself by your experiences. You may think to yourself; I'm worthless, I'm damaged, I'm unloved, I'm not social or nobody likes me. Do you embellish or focus on your perceived body imperfections? The list of negative self-talk you may use is endless. These negative self-definitions of your identity and your worth strongly impact the things that you do!

For example, some people start living life through fear and don't want to get hurt again so they avoid social situations. Sometimes women feel that they will always be powerless, hopeless and helpless to change their circumstances, so they give up trying to reach their dreams. There are moments when women are so angry about what happened to them that they direct the anger outward, toward others, or inward toward themselves. If you have turned your anger inward, then it is highly possible that you engage in behaviour that initially makes you feel better. However, over time this becomes harmful. Self-destructive behaviour can include suicidal behaviour, addictions, promiscuity and/or negative self-talk.

As a survivor of abuse, you may engage in a type of negative self-talk in which you tell yourself that you are what you've experienced. It is not your fault that you think in a negative or ungodly way. When you start defining yourself according to your negative experiences you are speaking to the death of yourself. Speaking death means you are using words that are hurtful and damaging to your spirit. Speaking death creates an atmosphere of failure, destruction and chokes the joy right out of your life. Speaking death to yourself is a negative coping strategy that you and many other women utilize as you try to make sense of your horrible experience(s). **You are not your experiences!** God revealed to me that when you define yourself according to your experiences, Satan is able to keep you from seeing the truth of who you are in God's eyes and prevents you from being the person God created you to be. The Bible is filled with scripture that speaks about how God sees you! Now grab a Bible and let's review some scripture so you can see the awesome things God says about you!

1. God sees you as His daughter. You are the daughter of the King of Kings!

"How great is the love the Father has lavished on us, that we should be called children of God! And that is what we are!" 1 John 3: 1

"Because those who are lead by the Spirit of God are *daughters* of God. For you did not receive a spirit that makes you a slave again to fear, but you received the spirit of *daughtership*." Romans 8:14-15 (Italic is my emphasis).

"The Spirit himself testifies with our spirit that we are God's children. Now if we are children, then we are heirs-heirs of God and co-heirs with Christ, if indeed we share in his sufferings in order that we may also share in his glory." Romans 8:16-17

2. God sees you as Righteous!

"Dear children, do not let anyone lead you astray. He who does what is right is righteous, just as he is righteous." 1 John 3:7

"God made him who had no sin to be sin for us, so that in him we might become the righteousness of God." 2 Corinthians 5:21

3. God sees you as Beautiful!

"And the fame spread among the nations on account of your beauty, because the splendor I had given you made your beauty perfect, declares the Sovereign Lord." Ezekiel 16:14

"Your beauty should not come from outward adornment, such as braided hair and the wearing of gold jewelry and fine cloths. Instead, it should be that of your inner self, the unfading beauty of a gentle and quiet spirit, which is of great worth in God's sight." 1 Peter 3:3-4

"To present her to himself as a radiant church, without stain or wrinkle or any other blemish, but holy and blameless." Ephesians 5:27

4. God sees you as Valuable!

"But God demonstrates his own love for us in this: While we were still sinners, Christ died for us." Romans 5:8

5. God sees you as having power and authority in Jesus name!

"In all these things we are more than conquerors through him who loved us." Romans 8:37

"You, dear children, are from God and have overcome them, because the one who is in you is greater than the one who is in the world." 1 John 4:4

6. He delights in you and wants to give you hope and a great future!

"The Lord will fulfill his purpose for me; your love, O Lord, endures forever—do not abandon the works of your hands." Psalm 138:8

"Being confident of this, that he who began a good work in you will carry it on to completion until the day of Christ Jesus." Philippians 1:6

"For I know the plans I have for you," declares the Lord, "plans to prosper you and not to harm you, plans to give you hope and a future." Jeremiah 29:11

"If the Lord delights in a *woman's* way, he makes *her* steps firm." Psalm 37:23

7. God is proud of you and highly esteems you!

"But you are a chosen people, a royal priesthood, a holy nation, a people belonging to God, that you may declare the praises of him who called you out of darkness into his wonderful light." 1 Peter 2:9

8. God sees you as very important so He sent His Son to die on the cross for you! He sacrificed His Son so that you can have eternal life!

"For God so loved the world that he gave his one and only Son, that whoever believes in him shall not perish but have eternal life." John 3:16

9. God forgets your mistakes and sees you as forgiven!

"For I will forgive their wickedness and will remember their sins no more." Hebrews 8:12.

10. God sees you as successful and strong!

"Before them the earth shakes, the sky trembles, the sun and moon are darkened and the stars no longer shines." Joel 3:10

11. God is committed to your success! You can succeed because His Spirit is within you!

"I can do everything through him who gives me strength." Philippians 4:13

12. God sees you as blessed and highly favored!

"The angel went to her and said, "Greetings, you who are highly favored! The Lord is with you." Luke 1:28.

13. God adopted you into His family. You are a child of God and you belong to Him!

"Yet to all who received him, to those who believed in his name, he gave the right to become children of God." John 1:12

14. God is proud of you!

"But you are a chosen people, a royal priesthood, a holy nation, a people belonging to God."
1 Peter 2:9.

15. You are loved by God and NOTHING can separate you from His love!

"Who shall separate us from the love of Christ? Shall trouble or hardship or persecution or famine or nakedness or danger or sword? As it is written: For your sake we face death all day long; we are considered as sheep to be slaughtered. No, in all these things we are more than conquerors through him who loved us. For I am convinced that neither death nor life, neither angels nor demons. Neither the present nor the future, nor any powers, neither height nor depth, nor anything else in all creation, will be able to separate us from the love of God that is in Christ Jesus our Lord." Romans 8: 35-39.

16. God sees you as a chosen and a wanted child. He rejoiced at your birth!

"For he chose us in him before the creation of the world to be holy and blameless in his sight. In love he predestined us to be adopted as his *daughters* through Jesus Christ, in accordance with his pleasure and will." Ephesians 1:4-5

17. God gives you the strength for every task or challenge!

"I can do everything through him who gives me strength." Philippians 4:13

"No temptation has seized you except what is common to man. And God is faithful; he will not let you be tempted beyond what you can bear. But when you are tempted, he will also provide a way out so that you can stand up under it." 1 Corinthians 10:13

Isn't it comforting to know that this is how God actually sees you, as His daughter? You belong to a loving and protective Father who sees only the best in you and He wants nothing but the best for you. As the scripture states, God adores you so much! He only sees your innocence. He sees you as perfect through His Son, Jesus. You may argue that you have imperfections and weaknesses but God sees past them. God sees you as amazing! He loves you and sees you as one of his treasured possessions—His daughter. 1 Corinthians 6: 19-20 reads, "Do you not know that your body is a temple of the Holy Spirit, who is in you, whom you have received from God? You are not your own; you were bought with a price. Therefore, honor God with your body." From this scripture, you can see that God sees your physical beauty quite differently than you probably do. When you see yourself the way God does, it will change your perspective of yourself, others and the world. View yourself as God sees you and live your life proud to be a child of God. You are fearfully and wonderfully made!

Through Christ's Eyes
ACTIVITY

Get a mirror and look at yourself. While looking at yourself in the mirror, use the scripture provided on pages 46 to 48 to speak life over yourself by saying aloud the various scripture to yourself using the template below:

Say: "I am not my experience(s). God says [*you insert scripture here*]....Therefore, I am [*finish the sentence*]!"

For example say: "I am not my experience(s). God says in Luke 1:28 the Lord is with me and I am highly favored. Therefore, I am blessed and highly favored. I am never alone."

How did you feel after you applied the scripture to yourself? Once you get into the habit of applying His Word to your life, you will learn to define yourself the way He sees you. On a daily basis repeatedly tell yourself the scripture from pages 46-48. Write the scripture on a piece of paper and post them on your fridge, bathroom mirror or on the window over your kitchen sink to help you memorize the scriptures. The psalmist says in Psalm 119:11, "I have hidden your word in my heart." This activity is very powerful as it will give you a daily reminder of how God sees you and will help to change how you think and speak about yourself. Once you truly start to see yourself though God's eyes, you will begin to see a change in how you feel about yourself and the world around you. It is important to develop a new picture of yourself that accurately reflects how God sees you. As a child of God, you are somebody going somewhere! Stop looking at the distorted picture of yourself that Satan wants you to see. No tear has ever been hidden from God's eyes. Every hurtful word said to you, or about you, has never missed His ears. He was there when you were abused and felt the pain you felt and grieved with you. Luke 12:6-7 says, God even sees and cares about the little sparrow, so think how much more He cares about you! Psalm 139:10 also tell us that God has not forgotten you. And even though it might not feel like it, He is still in control, holding you in the palm of His hand. By faith you must accept the reality of who you are in Jesus Christ and let God affirm you in your new identity. Shifting your eyes to see yourself as He sees you, requires that you see yourself full of potential and promise. God sees your greatness. He alone is the One who can reveal what is within you.

How you see yourself will determine how you act and carry yourself. It determines how you interact with others and how you perceive your self-worth. Satan wants you to see your failures, imperfections and bad circumstances. God wants you to see your future! Satan wants you to see your problems. God wants you to see your power! Step out in faith. Choose to see yourself the way God sees you. God sees you as reflecting His image of goodness and Glory. God says you are beautiful! You are unique! No two people are the same. No man can replicate the human eye, only God. When God looks at you, He sees His masterpiece. When you look in the mirror, the image looking back at you does not need alteration. In the book of Genesis, God creates, then calls His creation very good. God created you and He knitted you in your mother's womb (Psalm 139). God delights in his creation because He sees only good.

Whose identity are you in agreement with, Satan's or God's? It's important to live by your true identity in Christ. Try to see yourself through God's eyes and be more gentle, kind and gracious to yourself. God sees each of us through his eyes, not man's. God sees you through eyes of unconditional love and sees perfection manifested in you, His precious daughter!

PRAYER SAMPLE:

"Lord, I ask you to help me understand your love and vision of me so that I may love you more deeply, through this awareness of how you see me. I pray that I may also grow to love myself even more and accept who I am in your eyes. Lord, help me to replace my view of myself with how you see me. Lord, Psalm 19:10 and Isaiah 13:12 states, you see me as holy, righteous and more precious than the purest gold. Lord, thank you for showing me that I am not my mistakes. I am not my experience(s). Help me to see myself through your eyes. Lord, you said that I am _____ . [Put in scripture verse] When I start having negative thoughts that contradict Your Word, help me to stop. Lord, help me to speak life into myself and see the love you have for me. Lord, I am your precious daughter. You created me in your image of goodness and glory. You love me unconditionally. I am fearfully and wonderfully made! Amen."

HOMEWORK:
When you catch yourself having negative thoughts or speaking negatively about yourself and/or struggling with difficult emotions—speak aloud to yourself the word of God (use scriptures found on page 46-48) to remind you of how your Heavenly Father sees you!

CHAPTER TEN

Thinking Mistakes

MANY SURVIVORS OF SEXUAL ABUSE HAVE PATTERNS OF THINKING ABOUT THEMSELVES, OTHERS, OR THE world that contributes to a negative mindset. Your perception, or the way you think, may be distorted or incorrect because of the abuse which contributes to your poor self-worth, low self-image, decreased sense of belonging and low mood. Sometimes your thoughts are not true and in turn, do not help you feel better or solve your problems. You may be experiencing one or more *thinking mistakes*. Your inaccurate thinking patterns contribute to self-defeating behaviour which keep you stuck in negative thinking. Thinking mistakes are ungodly thinking patterns. It is not your fault that you have these thinking mistakes. These ungodly thinking patterns are not in alignment with the word of God. Phillipians 4: 8-9 states, "whatever is true, whatever is noble, whatever is right, whatever is pure, whatever is lovely, whatever is admirable-if anything is excellent or praise worthy-think about such things. Whatever you have learned or received or heard from me, or seen in me-put it into practice. And the God of peace will be with you." This scripture cautions you against this form of ungodly thinking pattern and identifies what a Godly thinking pattern is and the benefits of keeping your mind on God. God also encourages you to keep a sober-minded and stay alert. Let's look at 1 Peter 5:8-9a, it states, "Be self-controlled and alert. Your enemy the devil prowls around like a roaring lion looking for someone to devour. Resist him, standing firm in the faith." The scripture highlights that your mind can be a place for spiritual warfare. You can be unhappy, depressed, sad, or struggle to experience joy in your life because of a negative thinking pattern that was influenced from the trauma of sexual abuse and a dysfunctional past. A godly thinking pattern can help you cope more easily with daily concerns of life and bring optimism into your life, while helping you to avoid or minimize worry and negative thinking. Embracing a new thinking pattern will bring new changes into your life such as feeling happier and more successful. A Godly thinking pattern leads to happiness and success.

Godly thinking will change your outlook on life, the way you look at the world and the people around you. Romans 12:1-2 also encourages survivors to renew and restore their mind, "Therefore, I urge you *sisters (my emphasis)*, in view of God's mercy, to offer your bodies as living sacrifices holy and pleasing to God-this is your spiritual act of worship. Do not be conformed any longer to the pattern of this world, but be transformed by the renewing of your mind. Then you will be able to test and approve what God's will is-his good, pleasing and perfect will." This scripture highlights the attitude and actions God wants you to live out in your daily life. It's vitally important that renewing of our mind is a truth God intends for you to practice. These verses call you to make a commitment to live by a whole new way of thinking and behaving for the glory of God and to your good.

When you feel sad, angry, lonely or have a negative attitude; it is important to examine your thoughts and look for thinking mistakes that are contributing to these difficult feelings. What are you saying to yourself? You can identify an incorrect thinking pattern by asking yourself the following question; am I negatively judging my abilities or character? If so, you have thinking mistakes that are influencing your mood. According to David Burns (1998), all your negative thoughts are unhealthy thinking traps that distort your interpretation of things when you feel sad, angry, anxious, depressed, and/or stressed. David Burns (1998) suggests that there are several different thinking patterns that are unhealthy for your emotional well-being.

Can you relate to any of these? Put a cross next to each one that relates to you.

1. **All or Nothing Thinking** - You tend to perceive a situation/event in two categories and not on a continuum. You also only see things in extremes or absolutes. You see things in black and white with no gray areas. Example: If you receive a bad grade on a test, An All or Nothing thought might be: "I might as well drop out of the course because I'm not going to pass it anyway!"

2. **Yes But, Thinking** - You identify the positives in a situation but then quickly discount the positive by illuminating and focusing on the negative aspects of the situation. Example: A co-worker tells you that she likes your hairstyle. The Yes But, thinking might be: "Yes, she's just saying that to be nice, but really I'm having a bad hair day."

3. **Overgeneralized Thinking** - You make a conclusion about a negative situation continually happening to you, based on one or two small events. Example: You discover that the new girl in your book club doesn't like you. The Overgeneralized Thought might be: "No one likes me. I don't have any friends."

4. **Mind Reader Thinking** - You make assumptions about what people are thinking without checking with them. You fail to consider other more likely possibilities. You assume that people are thinking and behaving negatively toward you and often jump to conclusions without checking out the information to see if it's true.

5. **Predicting the Future** - You constantly predict something negative will happen to you in the near future without any evidence or considering other outcomes. You also think that things will not change for the better. Example: You are invited to a book club. The Predicting the Future thought

might be: "I won't have anything interesting to say, so I won't have fun and people will think I'm stupid." Then you turn down the invitation, making excuses why you are unable to attend.

6. **Should Statements:** You tell yourself how you should or must act. You have a precise, fixed belief of how you and others *should* behave and you negatively judge when expectations are not met. You criticize yourself. Your statements begin with "I should do this" "I should do that" "I should not" "I must" "I ought to" and "I have to." Example: After having several therapy sessions, you find you are still struggling to cope with your abuse. The Should Statement might be: "I should be over this by now." You judge your healing process negatively.

7. **Emotional Reasoning** - You decide that your bad feelings about a situation accurately reflect the truth of your situation. You decide how things really are based on how you feel. Example: You just finished writing a test that you were very nervous about writing. Someone asks you how the test went. The Emotional Reasoning might be: "I was so nervous during the test, I know I failed it. I'm so dumb."

8. **Labeling Thinking** - You say something negative about yourself or others. You are judgmental and only see the shortcomings of yourself and others. You call yourself and others names. Example: You forgot about your medical appointment. The Labeling Thinking might be: "I'm so stupid. I'm irresponsible." Instead of, "I forgot about the appointment. I will just have to rebook it."

9. **Personalizing** - You believe others are behaving negatively because of you, without considering alternative explanations for their behaviour. You take full responsibility for something you were unable to respond to. You may blame yourself for something in which you were not entirely responsible. You may blame other people without considering how you contributed to the problem. When personalizing, you may internalize or externalize an event. Example: Your spouse asks you for a divorce. The Personalizing thought might be: "I was not a good wife." You take full responsibility for the failed marriage, instead of exploring how he also contributed to the marital difficulties.

10. **Catastrophizing and Minimizing** - You exaggerate the likelihood that something bad will happen. You may exaggerate the degree of severity of something that has happened or how bad something would be if it really did happen. You tend to unrealistically magnify the negativity of the situation, while minimizing the positive. You may minimize the importance of a situation. Example: You received a complaint from a customer about your job performance. The catastrophic thought might be: "My boss will be upset. Customers are always right. I'm going to get fired!" You automatically assume you are getting fired before you know the nature of the customer's complaint.

To change your negative mood, you must first identify your negative thoughts. You have to acknowledge your distorted thinking pattern. Once you've identified the unhealthy thinking, you need to substitute it with a godly thought. You must replace lies with God's truth!

In the space below, take a few minutes and list the thinking mistakes you have.

_____

_____

_____

_____

_____

HOMEWORK:

Change the way you think!

Your thoughts can go unnoticed or undetected which often contributes to your belief system. Over the next few days take an inventory of the Thinking Mistakes that you are using. Follow the steps below to help you with this activity.

Step 1: Consciously pay attention to your thoughts.

Step 2: Write down the specific thinking mistake(s) you are using.

Step 3: Ask yourself: Are these thoughts helpful? Do these thoughts promote life? Do these thoughts build me up?

Step 4: Be a non-judgmental observer of your thoughts.

Step 5: Compare your thoughts to the scripture.

Step 6: Re-write your thinking mistakes into more helpful positive statements. Make sure it is aligned with the word of God.

Step 7: Practice saying the new statement aloud. If you practice, you can change your thoughts. If you say a negative thought about yourself 2000 times, then it became a habit that may be perceived as truth, but in reality is not. To counter, repeatedly tell yourself the re-constructed, Godly, truthful thought about yourself. When you first apply the Godly thought to yourself it may feel awkward and uncomfortable. Once you begin to believe the Godly statement to be a true reflection of you and implement your helpful behaviour, then you will see your mood elevate!

"be transformed by the renewing of your mind."

Romans 12:2

You have just finished learning various aspects about your thoughts which may require changing how you think. Let's review how to change your thoughts so you can put it into practice. Take a moment to review the sample Change Thought Chart below.

Change Thought Situation: Wendy feels nauseated when walking in the mall. She immediately tells herself, I'm going to be so embarrassed if I have a panic attack at the mall. In order for her to feel better she needs to change her negative, unhelpful thinking. What are helpful thoughts she can say to herself?

	BEHAVIOR	THOUGHT	FEELINGS
UNHELPFUL	Overthinking her symptoms	I'm going to have a panic attack. I'm such a loser!	Nausea, fear, panic, anxiety
HELPFUL	Thought Stopping technique* & Controlled breathing* & Relaxation	I'm okay! This feeling will only last a few minutes.	More in control Less anxious Less panicky

*See page 57 Thought Stopping & page 77 Controlled Breathing

Wendy was able to change her self-defeating thoughts with positive results. Wendy applied relaxation techniques, controlled breathing and re-framed her thoughts to manage her symptoms which led to an improved mood. It is important not to act on fear or panic, as it will only get worse in the long run.

Without using a specific incident of your abuse, take a moment to recall two non-traumatic situations that you were involved in recently such as, waiting in a long line up at the grocery store or giving a presentation at work. Next, using the Participant's Worksheet on page 56, write down the details of the situation. Then, fill in what you perceive as your unhelpful thoughts. Next re-write the thoughts into something that is more helpful and positive.

Participant's
WORKSHEET

Situation 1: Briefly explain the situation you experienced in the space below. Then complete the chart.

	BEHAVIOR	THOUGHT	FEELINGS
UNHELPFUL			
HELPFUL			

Situation 2: Briefly explain the situation you experienced in the space below. Then complete the chart.

	BEHAVIOR	THOUGHT	FEELINGS
UNHELPFUL			
HELPFUL			

THOUGHT STOPPING TECHNIQUE

Previously, you learned that your thoughts influence how you feel and how you behave. Your thoughts can sometimes ruminate or repeat in your mind. These repeated unhealthy thoughts can develop into unconscious automatic thoughts that lead to a significant decline in your mood. If your thoughts are focused on worry or doubt, it can lead to a sense of helplessness, anxiousness, low self-worth and/or a lack of confidence. Your behaviour mirrors your thoughts and feelings. An effective, yet simple technique to minimize the effects of negative, ruminating, intrusive thoughts on your mood is called thought stopping. This technique is often used with individuals struggling with anxiety, depression and panic disorders. It is also a great technique to use to reduce stress. This technique interrupts unhelpful, unwanted, negative thoughts and redirects you to think positively! Using a STOP directive will help remind you to focus on pleasant, life-giving thoughts. This gentle, verbal prompt is a distraction to allow you to gain control of your thoughts and promote a happier mood.

How to get started with the thought-stopping technique:

1. Identify unhelpful thoughts. Take inventory of the thoughts you are repeatedly thinking. Write them down. Are they positive or negative? Which thought is causing you the most stress?

2. When you find yourself focusing on a negative thought, silently shout STOP, to distract yourself from continually focusing on the unhealthy thought. Another way to distract yourself from thinking negative thoughts requires the use of a rubber band, scrunches or flexible bracelet on your wrist. Instead of using a verbal directive to stop, you can pull the rubber band, scrunches or bracelet to tap your wrist. Tapping the wrist will give you a gentle reminder that you need to refocus your thoughts. You can also put a small keepsake in your pocket to rub when you want to think of something more positive. The small keepsake could be a pendent, a special emblem or a small angel. The keepsake should have sentimental value and always promote positive feelings!

3. Once you have told yourself STOP, you need to replace the unhealthy thought with a gentle, truthful, life-giving thought. You are free to use scripture or other positive reinforcing thoughts.

4. Repeat this technique until it becomes automatic, to stop your thoughts from ruminating. It will help clear your mind of unwanted thoughts.

CHAPTER ELEVEN

A Victorious Mindset

"But thanks be to God! He gives us the victory through our Lord Jesus Christ"

1Corinthians 15: 57

NOW THAT YOU HAVE IDENTIFIED YOUR UNGODLY BELIEFS, IT'S TIME TO TAKE STEPS TO RENEW YOUR MIND. I believe that God has a better future for you than your past or your ungodly beliefs appear to speak! The truth creates the foundation for a godly belief system while a lie creates the foundation for an ungodly belief system. Ungodly beliefs keep you from spiritual maturity. Spiritual maturity requires that as a Christian, you learn to walk in obedience to God and make the choice to live by God's viewpoint rather than your human viewpoint. You are unable to grow in spiritual maturity unless you are in agreement with God. Spiritual maturity requires that you root out those things that are in disagreement with God, which prevent you from maturing and growing spiritually.

God calls on us to renew our mind! Romans 12:2 states, "Do not conform any longer to the pattern of this world, but be transformed by the renewing of your mind. Then you will be able to test and approve what God's will is—His good, pleasing and perfect will." Renewing your mind requires that you reject Satan's lies and come into agreement with God and His truth! To be victorious over your mind, you need to have a personal relationship with God and discover the truth of His word and what it says about you. When you discover the truth, it will be easier to recognize the ungodly beliefs that come into your mind and deal with them before they become part of your thought process.

Once a thought forms in your mind, positive or negative, it will bring about the law of sowing and reaping. The law of sowing and reaping means that every action and/or thought has a predictable consequence. Galatians 6:7-9 reads, "Do not be deceived: God cannot be mocked. A man reaps what he sows. The one who sows to please his sinful nature, from that nature will reap destruction; the one who sows to please the Spirit, from the Spirit will reap eternal life. Let us not become weary in doing good, for at the proper time we will reap a harvest if we do not give up." This scripture explains that everyone is a sower. As sowers, we will reap the harvest of what we sow. To illustrate this law, if you plant a rose seed and water it, it will grow into a beautiful rose bush. The same law has an impact on us in the spiritual realm and governs humanity. This law applies to all areas of our lives such as education, finances and our relationships with others.

As soon as an ungodly thought enters your mind, you have to take your thought captive immediately so it does not have a negative impact on you. Failure to take the thought captive will create an open door for Satan, to have access to your mind through all the lies you believe. Therefore, it is important to **replace** the lies that you believe about yourself with the truth from the word of God. Ask yourself: what is God saying about me in the scripture? You must then agree with what God says about you in the bible.

Now, let's agree in prayer to break the power of your ungodly beliefs and claim a victorious mindset in Jesus' name.

> *"Dear Lord Jesus, thank you for loving me unconditionally. Lord, help me to receive your love. Lord, I ask for your healing touch on the areas of hurt in my heart that led me to believe these lies. I repent and ask you to forgive me Lord, for receiving these ungodly beliefs. Lord, I choose to believe in your truth about me. I repent and ask for your forgiveness for living a life based on these ungodly beliefs and for the judgments I held of others because of my hurt. Heavenly Father, I receive your forgiveness. Thank you that I'm your child. Your Word says that no weapon formed against me shall prosper. I take authority over my mind, in Jesus' Name. Satan is a liar and I refuse to believe his lies about me, others or God. I have the mind of Christ. Lord, thank you, that you have not given me the spirit of fear, but of power, and of love and of a sound mind. God, help me to know who I am in Christ and who I'm meant to be. I put the cross between the ungodly belief and me so the ungodly belief has no impact. Lord, thank You that I have a mind of peace. I renounce and break my agreement with these ungodly beliefs. I choose to replace ungodly beliefs with godly beliefs. Lord, thank you for always being with me and giving me this revelation about ungodly beliefs. Heavenly father, thank you for helping to restore my mind. Lord, I choose to accept, believe and receive the godly beliefs that I am ____ [Fill in the blank].*

When you catch yourself having negative thoughts, immediately replace the ungodly thoughts with godly thoughts until the ungodly beliefs are destroyed. Repeatedly speak aloud over yourself, life-giving godly thoughts. Here are some life-giving, godly thoughts that you can use to replace ungodly thoughts.

"I am a winner!"……..2 Cor. 2:14

"I am an adequate person!"……2 Cor. 9:8

"I am unique and special!"…..1 Peter 2:9

"My life has purpose! ....Eph. 2:10

"I am successful!"....Psa.1:1-3

"God fights for me. I do not need to be afraid. With God standing with me, I am strong and able!"................Psa. 27:1

"I can do all things through Christ who strengthens me. He helps me to be sufficient for every task!"..... Phil. 4:13

"I will overcome every obstacle in my way!"....John 16:33

"I am secure and confident!".....Prov. 3:24-26

"Health and prosperity are mine!"....3 John 2

"God supplies all my needs. I do not need to worry about tomorrow because God is my provider!"........ Phil. 4:19

"I cast all my cares on Him, for He cares for me. I give all my worries to God!" ....1 Peter 5:7

"I am a totally new person!" ....2 Cor. 5:17

Now that you have learned how to renew your thoughts and claim a victorious mindset, let's put your learning into practice. Using the Godly Thought Worksheet on page 62, record on five different days, 5 different situations that you have experienced. Next to each situation, record the corresponding negative thought you had about yourself. Then, replace the negative thought with a realistic godly thought. To help you complete the chart on page 62, you can use scriptures, the Godly thoughts listed on pages 60-61 and/ or make up you own Godly thoughts.

Godly Thoughts
WORKSHEET

DATE	SITUATION	NEGATIVE THOUGHT	GODLY THOUGHT

MODULE THREE
Behavior

Changing Your Behavior

CHAPTER TWELVE

Counterfeit Affections

THERE ARE COMMON AND NORMAL RESPONSES TO SEXUAL ABUSE THAT YOU MAY EXPERIENCE. RESPONSES experienced by many survivors include feeling powerless, emotional numbness, denial, disturbed sleep, flashbacks, nightmares, loss of confidence, mood changes, low self-esteem, fear, and anxiety. Other symptoms could include, but are not limited to, depression, hostility, anger, sexual confidence or lack of sexual confidence, alienation, isolation, loss of control and feelings of emptiness or void.

Emptiness is an inner human experience. You may feel incomplete or feel something is missing within that prevents you from feeling contentment. This feeling of emptiness or some type of void, is one of the most pervasive and traumatic responses a survivor experiences because they intensify the feeling of being unloved. Do you feel unloved? How do you meet your need for love? Do you do things because you need to be needed? In order to fill the void or emptiness that was created by the abuse, you may seek comfort and identity through *counterfeit affections.*

According to Jack Frost (2006) in his book, Spiritual Slavery to Spirit of Sonship, counterfeit affections are power, possessions, position, people, places, performance or passions of the flesh. These things in themselves are not necessarily sin; however, the moment the pursuit of these things become more important than God and others, they become counterfeit affections or idols in your heart. God warns us against chasing after counterfeit affections in Ezekiel 14:4 and Matthew 6:21, 24. Jack Frost argues that the vicious cycle of chasing counterfeit affections will continue until you realize that these things will not satisfy you and your unmet need for intimacy and love. Counterfeit affections are those things that keep us from having an intimate relationship with God and prevent us from receiving the fullness of His love. What are you chasing after? What or who has become your idol?

God revealed to me that He will use whoever and whatever He wants to prove that He is enough! I further sensed God saying, He will do what He has to do to get your attention to prove His love for you. God is in the business of removing counterfeit affections out of your life! God will reveal your counterfeit affections and then deliver you from them. Your need for unconditional love will only be satisfied when you embrace your Heavenly Father's love. God's love will displace the pain of your abuse and change your life. Having counterfeit affections is not caused by lack of faith, weakness or insufficient willpower. Counterfeit affections can enter your heart very quietly. They allow you to manipulate and control situations and people. The pursuit of counterfeit affections will cause you to lose your connection with God. If you are disconnected from the Father's love and not resting in His ability to protect you, it prevents you from being a carrier of God's love to yourself, family, colleagues, church family and others you encounter in life.

To determine if you have a counterfeit affection, it is important to assess the condition of your heart and the motives behind your actions. Ask yourself: Is my heart open for love or closed to love? Are my motives pure? Impure motives involve trying to manipulate or control a situation to get what you want. Having a closed heart manifests as inability to forgive, anger outbursts, impatience, inability to stand up for yourself, destroying others around you, self-condemnation, rebellion against authority, competitiveness, limited respect for people, judging and criticizing others and fear of having intimate relationships. For instance, under the disguise of serving God, you may be spending countless hours serving in the church with the hope you will be accepted and gain status by being part of a specific group. Or, you may always take on additional responsibilities or projects at work hoping that you will receive a promotion. You may think the promotion will give you happiness and recognition from other people. Striving for acceptance and approval to feel loved by others is a sure sign that you do not have a revelation of God's love for you. A closed heart means that you are not in alignment with God.

An open heart manifests by freely giving away love without expecting something in return. For example, you may be patient and loving toward the store clerk who is short tempered and rude to you. An open heart says, "I'm okay and I'm going to give God's love away, even to those I believe don't deserve it." An open heart manifests when you are able to feel secure with whom you are as a child of God, even when you face failure and receive rejection from others. Having an open heart requires that you have healthy boundaries. Take a moment and check the condition of your heart. Are you open to receive and give love? You can be set free of counterfeit affections and become realigned with God when you embrace your heavenly Father's love!

Take a moment to list the ways you displayed a closed heart today? What got in the way of your giving your love away?

_____

_____

_____

Take a moment to list the ways you displayed an open heart today? What helped you to give your love away?

_____

_____

_____

CHAPTER THIRTEEN

Soaking In the Presence of God

IT IS NOT ENOUGH TO HAVE HEAD KNOWLEDGE OF GOD'S LOVE. ONLY A PERSONAL, INTIMATE ENCOUNTER with God's unconditional love will displace the pain in your heart and remove counterfeit affections from your life. Having a supernatural encounter with God's love will lead you to feel more complete and whole. Resting in the security of His love will allow you to be who you really are and live a life of fullness!

Once you have checked the condition of your heart, take some time to engage in the practice of soaking in the presence of God. Soaking is a term used to describe a spiritual meditation in which you spend time soaking (resting) in God's presence. Soaking will allow you to receive from the Lord, while you develop and enjoy a more intimate relationship with Him. It involves expectantly waiting to receive God's love. What you receive from the Lord will depend on the purpose of your soaking, which is different for each person. If you are sad and need comfort, then you should engage in soaking until you receive comfort and love from God. If you need help making a decision about a situation in your life, then soak until God gives you a word or revelation. Soaking can be done when you are happy or struggling with something. Soaking permits you to sit in the presence of God and have a physical reminder that He is alive and ever-present. As you rest and expectantly wait on the Lord, you will draw closer to Him and He will call your attention to words, visions, impressions, scriptures and answers to your prayers and questions. Waiting in the presence of God will help to quiet your spirit as you become filled with the Holy Spirit. Scripture says you have access to God. You don't need to be a preacher, a pastor or a high priest. God has given everyone access to Him, through Jesus, His Son.

"In Him and through faith in Him we may approach God with freedom
and confidence" Ephesians 3:12

> "Let us then approach the throne of grace with confidence, so that
> we may receive mercy and find grace to help us in our time of need."
> Hebrews 4:16

God created you to seek His presence, because in His presence is fullness of joy! The more you engage in soaking, the easier it is to experience the presence of God and it will increase your ability to hear from God. God does speak to His children. Many people don't hear from God because they are too busy and don't take the time to be still in His presence. Psalm 46:10 says, "Be still and know that I am God." Soaking will help you to be REALIGNED with God, as you allow His presence to wash over you so that He can restore and counsel you. Soaking will bring you through an exciting process of healing. When you pursue His presence by focusing your heart, spirit, mind and body on Him, you will experience God's presence. Focus on the things of God and not on this world. Time with God is necessary for a healthy spiritual life. Basking in the presence of God has led to restored relationships and marriages, people set free from addictions, healed of mental illness and lives transformed. Often we talk to God but don't listen to what he has to say. Soaking is only effective when you wait for God's response. It is a powerful tool for you to be able to listen to God answers to your difficult, yet honest and sincere questions regarding your experience of childhood sexual abuse.

Ten Simple Steps on How to SOAK in God's Presence:

1. Find a quiet place that is free from distractions like people, pets and noise. You can sit or lie down, whatever is most comfortable for you. Set aside 45 minutes for this activity.

2. Before you begin this activity, you need to decide on the purpose for your soaking. To help you decide here are some questions to ask yourself:
   What is the purpose of soaking for me?
   Is there something I want to talk to God about?
   Is there an area in my life I want God to heal?
   Do I want to spend time with God simply to enjoy His companionship?

3. Play some Christian music (gospel, worship or instrumental music) for a peaceful and fun atmosphere. You may start with three music selections you enjoy to help you dance before the Lord. Then play more gentle music as a backdrop that will help you to surrender yourself to God when you do this activity. The music is to help you to create an atmosphere that is inviting for God. You are welcoming God to come be with you, just as you would a guest you invite to your home.

4. Repent of any sin you may have in your life and ask for God's forgiveness. You do not ask forgiveness for the sin that was done to you. This step allows you to go before God with a pure heart.

5. Invite the Holy Spirit into Soaking time. Say repeatedly, "Come Holy Spirit, come."

6. Worship the Lord by offering a prayer of thanksgiving and/or adoration.

7. Create an attitude of expectancy by recalling the many ways God has manifested His power and miracles. Recall the various miracles performed by Jesus.

8. Then repeatedly say, "Lord, I want more of your presence." Keep yourself quiet and still. Wait on the Lord to come. As you wait for Him, keep yourself focused on Him. Psalm 37:7 says, *"Be still before the Lord and wait patiently for him."*

9. During this quiet time, begin to talk with God about whatever you desire. Here are some questions to guide you during this period:

   What do you need from God concerning a situation in your life?

   If you need guidance during your devotional time, open your bible and ask the Lord what verse or chapter He wants you to read?

   Did the Lord give you a vision, an impression, brought to mind a person or place? Ask Him, why He gave the vision, impression, person, place or situation to you? Does He want you to pray for a specific person or situation?

10. Now be still and listen to what God has to say to you! Jesus said, "I am He who searches hearts and minds (Revelation 2:23).

This spiritual meditation requires that you wait and be still before the Lord. You do not come out of the soaking until you receive a revelation for the purpose of your soaking. Many people miss out on the blessing of fellowship with Jesus because they lost the ability or fail to cultivate the ability to recognize His voice. Jesus said, "My sheep listen to my voice; I know them and they follow me." Many survivors are hungry for the intimate relationship with God that can satisfy the desires of their hearts. The more time you spend practicing the presence of God, the more you will increase the level of intimacy in your relationship with Him. As you increase in intimacy with God, you will get to know him more personally as He imparts his love over you. Is your heart feeling empty? Posture yourself in Jesus Christ and receive his love. God will fill your heart with His love and transform your identity!

CHAPTER FOURTEEN

Assertive Communication

"There is a time for everything, and a season for every activity under heaven."

Ecclesiastes 3:1

THE DEEP BELIEFS WOMEN HOLD AS A RESULT OF THE ABUSE THEY HAVE EXPERIENCED CAN IMPACT HOW they communicate with others. These negative, deep-seated beliefs about themselves contribute to a lack of assertiveness, which can create power struggles in relationships and reinforce inequalities, inequity and oppression in relationships. Communicating effectively using assertive techniques can improve self-esteem. Enhancing one's self-esteem requires changing defeating, negative thinking and behaviour patterns in your communication style. Assertive communication will help you stay calm in difficult conversations, decrease aggressive behaviour, help you successfully communicate your feelings, thoughts and opinions, stand up for yourself and no longer be pushed around. It will improve your self-worth! Whenever Jesus spoke, He spoke with assertiveness. Jesus did not speak with aggression or passivity. Passivity and aggressiveness comes from fear and false pride—Jesus had neither of these.

Assertiveness will give the message that you are confident and have self-control. Assertive communication will allow you to earn respect from your peers and help you say no without fear or worry about what others may think of you. It allows you the ability to create personal boundaries. Assertive communication will enhance your relationships, reduce anxiety and stress. It will help you to promote balance, handle difficult family, friends, and coworkers, reducing chaos and drama in your life. By asserting self-love and appreciation as well as accepting yourself regardless of your imperfections, you reflect the confidence of who you are in Christ. Assertive communication helps you to talk and walk with excellence! You are a woman of Excellence!

ASSERTIVE COMMUNICATION STRATEGIES

Use of I messages:

If you start a statement with **I** instead of **you, it** allows you to express yourself without judging or placing blame. **I** statements help to minimize blaming statements toward others and the display of intense emotions when you talk. If you begin a statement with **you**, it will contribute to the other person being defensive and have their back up, even though that was not your intent. Starting your sentence with **I** allows the other person to be more in tune to what you are saying to them, more focused on how you are feeling and how you are affected by their behaviour. Using "I" statements helps the other person to focus on problem solving, while maintaining the integrity and dignity of both people in the conversation. Using **I** messages shows that you are taking ownership of your words and your reactions.

Example of You Message: "You never help with the dishes."
I statement: "I feel appreciated when you help with the dishes and share the household chores."

Below are **I** statements scripts you can use when talking with others:

"I feel…."
"I believe…"
"I think…"
"I want…"
"I need…"
"I don't…."
"I am not willing…"

When/Then Statements:

These statements allow you to set up boundaries when interacting with others, while eliciting their co-operation. To effectively use this technique, it's important to focus on the behaviour of the other person, your feelings and to establish your personal boundaries.

Example of Unhelpful statement: "Stop getting in my face!"
Assertive statement: "When someone violates my personal space, I get angry!" or "When my personal space is respected, then I feel more comfortable engaging in conversation."

OR

Unhelpful statement: "You're late again for our meeting! You are inconsiderate!"
Assertive statement: "When you're late, it shows my time is not important to you, and then I feel angry."

Here is the formula for this strategy:
"When my [other person's behaviour], then I feel [insert your feeling, or action you will take].

Refrain from Criticism:
It's very easy for us to judge another person's behaviour and opinions that are not in line with our own. In addition, when people are self-critical and lack confidence, they are quick to label their own behaviour negatively. Assertive communication requires that you speak about your own behaviour and the behaviour of others in a non-judgmental way. It requires that you do not criticize or negatively judge someone's character because you disagree with his/her position.

1. Unhelpful statement: "I'm so stupid. I don't have enough money to pay my phone bill because I overspent on groceries."
Assertive statement: My groceries cost more than I planned, so I will have to reassess my budget to include my phone bill."

2. Unhelpful statement: "You're late again for our meeting! You are inconsiderate!"
Assertive communication: "We were scheduled to meet at 9:30 a.m. It is now 10 a.m. I can only meet for 30 minutes as I have another appointment."

Assertive Godly statements require the individual to insert scripture that speaks life to them and promotes a positive outlook. God says, [you insert scripture here]. I am capable of [list your ability here].
Unhealthy statement: "I'm so stupid. I spent too much money."
Godly statement about yourself: "God says I am of sound mind. I know how to manage my money with His help."

Active Listening:
Active listening is a way of listening and responding to another person that will promote mutual understanding in conversations. Active listening requires you to be present in the here and now with the other person. Being present requires that you do not offer rebuttals, no defensive replies-- you focus solely on what you heard! When talking to someone it's important to listen to what they have to say and then repeat back what you think you heard. Repeating and paraphrasing what you think you heard the other person say, creates an opportunity for the person to revise the message they are trying to send or confirm that you heard correctly. To ensure you understand the other person's perspective, it is important to ask questions to confirm that you understood the other person's position. Be willing to negotiate and be flexible on some topics of discussion.

Unhealthy: "You are not listening to me. That is not what I said."
Assertive communication: "What I hear you saying is [paraphrase what you heard]. Did I hear you correctly?"

Reiterate Your Position Technique:

This technique is effective when dealing with someone who is persistent in trying to get you to do something you don't want to do or to pressure you **into** agreeing with their position. You simply restate your position using the exact same words each time. This technique will allow you to assert your position without losing control of your emotions.

Example interaction between parent and teenager:

Teenager: "Can I stay out until 1:30 a.m.?"
Parent: "Your curfew is 10 p.m. I expect you to keep your curfew."
Teenager: "Let's make a deal. I will come in next weekend at 9 p.m. if you let me stay out until 1:30 a.m."
Parent: "Your curfew is 10 p.m. I expect you to keep your curfew."
Teenager: "I will do extra chores, if you let me stay out late tonight."
Parent: "Your curfew is 10 p.m. I expect you to keep your curfew."

Body Language:

Assertive communication requires that you be mindful of the message you send with verbal and non-verbal communication. Body language also gives the message of how you want to be treated. Assertive body language will reinforce the other communication strategies, and will show that you respect yourself and others. These techniques will help you to reflect confidence.

• Ensure your voice is firm, pleasant and calm.

• Give firm handshakes.

• Say "umm," and nod your head to show you are listening.

• When talking with someone, ensure you are looking directly at them (eyes to eyes & face to face).

• Stand and sit straight (your shoulders should be back and not slouched).

• Have a friendly facial expression that says I'm open to talk to you. (Have a slight smile instead of frown or blank expression).

• Be mindful of thinking mistakes!

• Ensure the clothing you wear is clean, pressed, free of holes, wrinkles and stains to give you the look of confidence. You do not have to have designer brand name clothing to look confident!

Here are three different scenarios. Choose a scenario and practice using one of the assertive communication techniques. If possible, find someone you trust and respect to help you do a short role-play to practice using the new skills you have learned.

Role-Play #1: Someone is asking to borrow $100 from you. The person knows you have the money, but you want to save it for a rainy day.

Role-Play #2: You purchase a pair of jeans. You return home and notice there is a small hole on the inseam. You want a full refund for the jeans.

Role-Play #3: You are asked to take on another project at work and have it done by the end of the day. You realize this request is unrealistic but worry about the consequence if you refuse to do the additional project.

CHAPTER FIFTEEN

Controlled Breathing Technique

SURVIVORS OF TRAUMA OFTEN REACT TO THE TRAUMA MEMORIES WITH A STRESS RESPONSE. SOME symptoms of your stress response may be rapid heart rate, rapid breathing, clenching of teeth, sweaty palms, irritability, difficulties concentrating and sleeping. Survivors may also find themselves struggling with negative thinking patterns, nightmares, mentally reliving the sexual abuse or other triggers leading to a state of hyper alert, accelerated heart rate, and shallow breathing. This state of hyper alert may become the norm for survivors, thus contributing to anxiety and panic disorders. When you are feeling anxious, you tend to breathe shallow, using upper chest muscles which cause your breathing to become extremely rapid and erratic, leading to hyperventilation, increasing anxiety and the frequency and duration of panic attacks.

Controlled breathing is a method to counter the stress response and create a state of calm within a few minutes, enabling you to cope with stressful thoughts and situations. Survivors can eliminate or reduce these feelings of anxiety and panic by learning how to concentrate on their breathing. Controlled breathing provides a distraction from negative thoughts and is a method of relaxation when facing a stressful situation. Your breathing is directly related to tension within your body.

Our thoughts can directly impact our breathing. If you think about something distressing, your heart rate and breathing speeds up or becomes very shallow. If you think of something relaxing your breathing slows down. Controlled breathing techniques teach your mind to slow down and allow your body to immediately respond to your emotions such as fear, anxiety, worry or anger. Managing your breathing helps to reduce the heart rate and increase oxygen flow in the body. Controlled breathing focuses on diaphragmic breathing. Breathing through the diaphragm can transform a person's physical and psychological state by activating the areas of the brain responsible for relaxation. It's best to practice controlled breathing during times when stress levels are very low or non-existent. Practicing controlled breathing on a regular basis will help to develop a very effective way of controlling and coping with anxiety, panic attacks and hyperventilation. Controlled breathing is highly effective with arousal management.

Throughout the scripture, there are many incidents in which God breathes and brings things to life. Genesis 2:7 gives you an account of how heaven and earth was created. When the Lord created man kind, scripture indicated that "the Lord God formed the man from the dust of the ground and breathed into his nostrils the breath of life, and the man became a living being." In this scripture, breathe is equated with life. There are many references to breath or breathe in the bible, God is described as the giver of breath and life to animals, man and dead things. Breath is used in the bible as a symbol for God's life giving presence. Breathing shows your vulnerability and your total dependence on God. When you do this breathing activity visualize God breathing the breath of life in you and through you. When you breathe out, release everything that is not of God and is holding you back.

Guidelines for doing the controlled breathing technique:

1. Place one hand on your chest and one hand behind your back (just above your pant line). Placing one hand behind your back helps to keep your shoulders back so you can have proper body positioning.

2. Breathe in slowly….breathe in the Breath of God. Breathe in God's pure love. Observe the movement of your chest. It should be moving up. Let the peace of God be upon you. Breathe in for a count of four.

3. Observe your abdomen; it should be moving in or deflating slowly like a balloon.

4. Then, breathe out very slowly….breathe out all your worries and fears…giving your problems to God. Exhale all your tensions and contaminations. Observe the movement of your chest. Your chest should be moving downward. Observe your abdomen; it should be slowly filling with air like a balloon. Breathe out for a count of four.

5. Once you have learned this breathing technique, add a word that will help to keep your thoughts and mind calm as you breathe. Continue to breathe, but each time you breathe out say the relaxing word aloud or quietly. Examples of relaxing words that can be used are: calm, relax, slow, peace.

6. If you are breathing too fast and shallow, you will feel tension in your body. If you breathe deeply and slowly, you will feel relaxed.

7. Practice breathing this way at least three times per day, when you are under little or no stress. This technique can be done while standing or sitting, with your eyes open or closed.

CHAPTER SIXTEEN

No More Nightmares

SOME SURVIVORS OF ABUSE STRUGGLE WITH NIGHTMARES. NIGHTMARES CAN OCCUR REPEATEDLY WITHOUT A theme or the content may change but have a recurring theme such as being pursued or attacked. Nightmares can be a sign that you may have unresolved areas in your healing. Occasional nightmares are normal for survivors; however, consistent and frequent nightmares may mean you are overwhelmed or experiencing considerable stress. Often nightmares are accompanied by distressing emotions that identify and intensify your anxiety and fears, but can be a resource to learn about your insecurities, feelings of inadequacy, health worries, relationship difficulties or unresolved issues related to the abuse. Many survivors see nightmares as something over which they have little or no control. Applying these techniques will allow you to control your thoughts, just as you do when you are awake.

To prevent nightmares it is important to ensure you have healthy sleep. Maintaining healthy sleep hygiene practices requires you to engage in relaxing activities before going to bed. Dr. Jon Fleming, MD (2011) suggests that sleep hygiene involves not drinking caffeine after 4 p.m. and avoiding strenuous physical exercise after 6 p.m. Do not consume alcohol within 2 hours before bedtime. He also suggests avoiding naps during the day and getting up at the same time each morning, including weekends. Be mindful of the type of movies or books you engage in prior to going to bed. If you are having nightmares, refrain from reading and watching horror stories, especially on spiritual warfare. To have a healthy sleep you need to establish a consistent daily routine to train your body to know when it is time to sleep. For example, one hour before bed, you may Soak in the Presence of God or take part in reading/meditating on Scripture like Psalm 23. Other calming activities may include listening to spiritual music (lyrical or instrumental) to help you relax before you go to sleep to reduce nightmares.

With God's help you have the power to change your dreams! Changing your dreams while you are awake can dramatically reduce and eliminate nightmares. You must remember a nightmare is a story that can be rewritten any way you want. You can change any aspect of the dream that you desire. Changing your dreams is a process that will help you to be more aware of your dream time and create change while you are in a dream state. Trying to change your dreams while you are still asleep is not recommended to stop nightmares. The benefits of dream change while you are awake will help you be more skilled at changing dream images within the dream state. Changing your dreams will allow you to be in control of your thoughts while you are awake and in a dream state.

How to change your dreams:

1. Change your reaction to the dream. Often the reaction to nightmares is fear and worry. Don't give into the negative emotions rather focus your energy on positive feelings. Remind yourself that you are okay and you are safe; and you just had a nightmare. Remind yourself you are safe in God's embrace. When you awake from a nightmare, immediately sit up on the side of your bed, move your feet around and then do a visualization technique or soaking activity and controlled breathing to call yourself into the present. *(See Chapter 13 for Soaking Activity and Chapter 18 for Visualization Techniques)*.

2. Change the content or the ending of your dream to be positive by inviting God into your dream and creating a new dream image. While doing this activity it is important to utilize your controlled breathing technique. To create a spiritual dream image, you can be very creative with incorporating various elements into your dream by answering these questions. What do you want God to do? How do you want Him to help you? Where is God in your dream? What is God doing to protect you? What is God saying to you? Are there other biblical characters you want in your dream image?

3. When you invite God into your dream you can ask Him to change any aspect of the dream image and help you accomplish anything you need to in the dream, such as not turning a corner, finding a safe hiding spot or shrinking a monster. You can have God give you a tool, instrument or a certain person in your dream to change the outcome. For example, God can make you confident and fearless where previously in the nightmare you were scared and hopeless. Remember you and God are working in partnership to overcome your nightmares.

4. When dealing with recurrent nightmares that appear to have a theme, again invite God into your dream and/or ask Him the following questions:
What is the message you want me to have? What area in my life do you want to heal? He will answer you. While doing this activity it is important to utilize your controlled breathing technique.

5. Spend time writing down how you want the content or the ending of the dream image to change. This will help you recall your new dream image while you are in a dream state. Make sure you are using your controlled breathing technique for this activity.

6. Take a moment to write down in a dream journal, include the details of your dreams that you have been struggling with in the past few weeks or create a dream diary using the sample provided

below. Share your dream with a support person. Sometimes talking about your dreams is helpful. Discuss with your support person, your interpretation of the dream and your feelings surrounding the dream. Also share with your support person--Why do you think you are having this particular dream?

MY DREAM DIARY

DATE & TIME	DREAM DETAILS & YOUR REACTION	NEW CONTENT & YOUR REACTION

CHAPTER SEVENTEEN

Freedom From Flashbacks & Triggers

MANY SURVIVORS OF ABUSE EXPERIENCE FLASHBACKS AND/OR TRIGGERS THAT PULL THEM BACK TO THE TIME of the abuse, as if it was happening all over again. Flashbacks are involuntary, normal, recurrent memories of a previous traumatic event. Flashbacks can be caused by body sensations, things you see, sounds, tastes or smells. A trigger is a reminder of a traumatic event. Even though the trigger itself is not traumatic or threatening, it calls the survivor of abuse to remember a traumatic memory or experience of the abuse. Triggers place the person psychologically back to the time or specific incident of abuse. Triggers make the person feel as if they are re-experiencing the abuse.

As a survivor of abuse it is important to have insight into what your triggers are so that you can create emotional safety for yourself when you are triggered. Being able to identify your triggers will help you to manage your emotions and promote your healing. Traumatic memories are stored in your brain and can be triggered at any moment. Triggers are very personal and different for each individual. The senses are common triggers that can make you have an intense emotional reaction that is similar to the time of the sexual abuse. According to the Sexual Assault Center of Alberta (2008), triggers are diverse and are activated by one or more of the senses:

Sight:
- someone may resemble the abuser or has similar characteristics or objects such as sports jacket, hairstyle

- witnessing a situation in which someone else is being abused, such as how a person raises their eye brow or a verbal comment

- seeing an object that is similar to one that was used when you were abused

- seeing common objects in the home that are associated with or were common in the household where the abuse took place

    • any place or occasion where the abuse took place such as a water park, camp site, family or social event, holiday, birthday celebration

Sounds:

    • anything that sounds like anger, such as raised voices, bangs, loud noises, something breaking

    • anything that sounds like pain or fear, such as crying, screaming

    • anything that might have been in the location or situation before, during or after the abuse such as sound of a cat, music, car door closing

    • anything that resembles what the abuser did such as laughter, tone of voices, foot steps, opening of a can

    • words of abuse such as insults, put downs, labels, cursing

Smell:

    • anything that resembles the smell of the abuser such as cigarettes, alcohol, food, perfume, shaving cream

    • any smell that resembles the place or situation such as food, odors

Touch:

    • anything that resembles the abuse or anything that happened before, during or after the abuse such as a specific physical touch, someone standing too close, petting of an animal, the way someone approaches you

Taste:

    • anything that is related to the abuse, prior to the abuse or after the abuse, such as certain foods, alcohol, tobacco

Take a moment and think about the different triggers you have. Are you able to identify your triggers in each category? Take a minute to write down your triggers in the area below.

My **SIGHT** triggers are:

My **SOUND** triggers are:

My **SMELL** triggers are:

My **TOUCH** triggers are:

My **TASTE** triggers are:

Flashbacks may feel frightening, but are not dangerous to you. It is important to develop an attitude of acceptance and be non-judgment toward your flashbacks. Experience the flashbacks as if they are a normal part of your healing. Do not try to stop them, over think about them or keep them a secret. Talk with a support person such as spouse, friend or therapist about your flashbacks. When you have a flashback use relaxation, controlled breathing (chapter 15), repeatedly state a godly thought (chapter8), visualization (chapter 18) or another strategy you learned in this workbook to help you cope. You may also want to keep a Flashback Diary. Here is a sample Flashback/Trigger Diary that you may want to use. The diary is to capture the coping strategy that was most effective when you dealt with the flashbacks.

FLASHBACK/TRIGGERS DIARY:

DATE & TIME	TRIGGERS	FLASHBACK DETAILS	FEELINGS	WORRIES OR JUDGMENT ABOUT THE FLASHBACK	COPING STRATEGY

CHAPTER EIGHTEEN

Visualization Techniques

VISUALIZATION TECHNIQUES ARE HELPFUL TOOLS TO USE WHEN YOU ARE EXPERIENCING FLASHBACKS, nightmares and triggers. Visualizations are a technique of focusing your imagination on behaviour or events that have occurred in your life or that you want to achieve. Visualizations are created using a detailed representation of a past happy memory or your future goal. The visualization technique incorporates the different senses. Most importantly, this technique promotes the connection and balance between the mind and the body. By regularly focusing on comforting images and/or memories, visualization can change negative emotions and have a positive effect on your body. They can help to shift your attitude and create a sense of peace, harmony and happiness.

Visualize the Good:

1. Start by making yourself comfortable in a sitting or lying position.

2. Close your eyes and focus on your breathing. Inhale slowly and deeply through your nose for a count of three and exhale slowly through the mouth for a count of three. Repeat for four full breaths. Remember, your stomach should fill and empty like a balloon being filled and emptied of air.

3. Take a moment to visualize a previous accomplishment or a very happy moment in your life. Let your mind focus on this memory as you answer these questions. Where are you? Who are you with? What made this moment such a happy memory for you?

4. While you are focusing on this happy time in your life, take a few minutes to recall all the details about the memory using your five senses of Touch, Sight, Taste, Smell, and Hearing (TSTSH). The more details you can recall, the more effective the technique.
   Use these questions to help you recall details.
   Touch: What do you feel? Describe the different textures of what you felt.

Sight: What do you see? Describe everything you see in as much detail as you can.

Taste: Do you remember any tastes? List the various tastes which you can recall.

Smell: What do you smell? List all the smells you can recall.

Hearing: What do you hear? Say aloud all the things you hear.

5. Now rest and relax in the moment of peace you have created.

6. Optional: Create your own visualization and record it on an electronic device with your own voice so you can listen to it whenever you like.

Safe Place Visualization:

Visualizations promote healing by creating your own **safe place,** like a spiritual haven. You can do this safe place technique whenever you feel sad, angry, anxious, restless or afraid. You can return to this place in your imagination whenever you need to feel safe, relaxed and secure.

When you are first learning to do this exercise, it's very important to be in a quiet room, free of distractions and noise like cellular phones. This activity will take approximately 20 minutes. If you desire, you can make a voice recording of the steps to guide you along.

Creating a Safe Place:

Think of a real or imaginary place that makes you feel safe, such as the beach, a park or a specific room or building.

Next, you identify your safe place. My safe place is _____. In your imagined or real safe place, pray and invite God to be present in your space or ask God to send a multitude of angels to surround your safe place. Whatever you need to make your place safe!

Then, you can choose to keep your eyes open or closed--whatever is most comfortable for you. Inhale slowly and deeply through your nose for a count of three and exhale slowly through the mouth for a count of three. Repeat for four full breaths. Breathe in God's pure love. Remember your stomach should fill and empty as if it was a balloon being filled and emptied of air. Continue to breathe slowly as you engage in this activity.

Now with your eyes open or closed, imagine a set of stairs going down to your safe place. Focus on the warmth, love and peace you feel in God's presence. You are safe in God's strong embrace. You are standing on the top step and can see five more steps. Imagine yourself walking down the stairs to your safe place. As you walk down the stairs, imagine yourself holding onto God's hand. He won't let you go! Count yourself down five steps. Step five, Step four, Step three, Step two, and Step one. You are now at the entrance of your safe place. Enter!

What do you see? Is it daytime or night? Are you alone or with others? Describe what your safe place looks like. Now keep looking and enjoy your surroundings!

What are you doing in your safe place? Pay attention to the feeling of happiness that you have as you engage in this activity. Stay in that feeling of happiness for a few minutes.

Now take a few more minutes to look around your safe place and enjoy the moment of peace and comfort. Notice the warmth, safety and security of being in God's presence. Recognize how safe and relaxed you feel there. While in your safe space, speak aloud to remind yourself: "I'm okay and free of all my worries. In my safe place no one can harm me!"

Okay, when you are ready to leave your safe place, look around one last time to remember what it looks like and how you feel in your safe space. If you are ready to leave your safe place, you first need to climb the stairs that brought you to your safe place. Imagine yourself holding onto God's hand as you walk up the stairs. Count the steps as you slowly climb the stairs. Keep your eyes closed while you go up the stairs. Step one, Step two, Step three, Step four, and Step five. You are now at the top of the stairs. Focus on your breathing and notice how calm and relaxed you are. Take a few more breaths and open your eyes!

Optional: If you have a souvenir of your real safe place such as a rock from a beach you visited, you can place it nearby so that it can help you focus on this activity. The souvenir must be an object that creates positive emotions for you. If it has any negative attachment to people or events do not use the souvenir.

You have just learned many ways to modify behaviour that is influenced by your thoughts. As mentioned earlier, there is an interrelationship between your thoughts, behaviour and feelings/body sensations. Changing your behaviour will promote restoration and healing. Review the Sample Changing Behaviour chart below. This sample demonstrates that it is necessary to change your habits and adopt new ones. Ann changed her behaviour which contributed to changes in her thoughts and her mood.

Changing Behaviour Situation: Ann was feeling sad because she believed no one liked her. So she did not try to make friends. In order for her to feel better she would have to change her negative, unhelpful behaviour.

	BEHAVIOR	THOUGHT	FEELINGS
UNHELPFUL	Ann doesn't try to make friends [isolating behavior]	No one likes me. What a loser.	Sad, lonely, unhappy, afraid, shy
HELPFUL	Ann introduces herself to someone and learns they have many things in common	I'm friendly I'm easy going. I can make friends. I have interesting things to talk about. People do like me.	More in control, happy, hopeful, excited

You can see that when Ann changed her behaviour, her thoughts and feelings also changed to something much more positive.

Using the Participant's Sheet on page 91, think of two situations you have experienced recently. Complete the behaviour column of the chart. What were the situations? What was your unhelpful behaviour? How can you change your behaviour to be more helpful and positive next time? If you have time, complete the rest of the chart.

Participant's
WORKSHEET

Situation 1:

	BEHAVIOR	THOUGHT	FEELINGS
UNHELPFUL			
HELPFUL			

Situation 2:

	BEHAVIOR	THOUGHT	FEELINGS
UNHELPFUL			
HELPFUL			

CHAPTER NINETEEN

Godly Relationships

MANY SURVIVORS OF ABUSE FIND THEMSELVES IN FRAGMENTED, UNHEALTHY, OR BROKEN RELATIONSHIPS. The pattern of people coming and going out of their lives can leave them feeling confused, unloved, unwanted or that they are to blame. Disappointment in relationships can be painful.

If you are struggling to maintain friendships and/or long lasting relationships (with Christians and/or non-Christians), then it's important to evaluate your strategies for entering into relationship with people. So often survivors go into relationships trying to be what they think the other person wants them to be; which is a common and dangerous approach to relationships. Roy Croft says, "I love you not because of who you are, but because of who I am when I am with you." Roy Croft encourages people to perceive relationships by how you feel when you are around certain people.

Do the people in your life make you feel good about who you are or do they bring you down? Do you work harder to maintain the relationship than the other person? Do they inspire you to achieve the dreams God ordained for you? Do you feel relaxed and free to be yourself when with them? Do you hold onto unhealthy relationships out of fear of being alone?

This section on godly relationships will empower you to build emotional resiliency and healthy interpersonal relationships. God created you to be intimately connected with Him and those around you. Applying these strategies will move you away from dysfunctional relationships to discover and enjoy lasting relationships like God designed.

SEVEN CHARACTERISTICS OF GODLY RELATIONSHIPS

Alliance made with other people who love God:

Are you in relationship with people who love God? Are you in relationship with people who try to live a life pleasing God?

For relationships to function effectively, they must be built on the foundation of God's principles. All relationships (marriages, family, friendships, work relationships, neighbors, and church fellowship) must have their roots in Godliness.

In Ecclesiastes 4:9-12 it says,
> Two are better than one, because they have a good return for their labor: If either of them falls down, one can help the other up. But pity anyone who falls and has no one to help them up. Also, if two lie down together, they will keep warm. But how can one keep warm alone? Though one may be overpowered, two can defend themselves. A cord of three strands is not quickly broken.

This scripture is often used to describe marriages and friendships; however, it speaks about all interpersonal relationships. It highlights the foundation and key factors for a deeper relationship where each one is willing to help the other. Interdependence on each other and loyalty is essential to mutually defend one another. The scripture also teaches that two people bound together in Christ, are stronger than the individuals themselves. Relationships are more than a union of two individuals. With God at the center of the relationship (the third cord), your relationship will be strong and not so easily destroyed. This scripture confirms that God will perform a miracle in your relationship, uniting you and the other person together in a covenant relationship with Him as one.

Godly relationships require that all parties in the relationship (i.e. friendships, co-workers) encourage one another. Each party puts the other person before themselves and thus the relationships thrive. Each individual in the relationship must be confident in who they are and work together to achieve individual and mutual goals. To maintain relationships, all parties must work together as a team to provide protection against Satan's attacks and develop a reliance on each other. Satan can not break what God has knit together! Keep God at the center of all your relationships. Any relationship that ignores God's laws may be destined to be short-lived. Godly relationships are enjoyed because people have an understanding of God's love and are living out their lives by walking in His love. Love is not selfish, but puts the other first. God designed relationships to be conducted within the love of God.

Be mindful of things that draw you to connect with people:

Are you creating alliances with the right people? Amos 3:3 says, "Can two walk together, except they agreed?" It is your responsibility to protect your heart! Ellen Bass & Laura Davis (2008) in their book, Courage to Heal, remind survivors that, "It is necessary to structure your life so that you are in contact with people who respect you, who understand and take you seriously. This is what you did not have as a child and what you need now in order to construct healthy feelings of self-worth. It is important to stop being with people who make you feel bad about yourself." Godly relationships require that you be mindful of those things that draw you to create an alliance with people. What kind of things do you have in common with the people around you? Scripture warns you to be careful in choosing your friends.

"Be sure of this: The wicked will not go unpunished, but those who are righteous will go free." Proverbs 11:21

"The LORD detests all the proud of heart. Be sure of this: They will not go unpunished." Proverbs 16:5

Any relationship between individuals based on negative factors will not maintain a long-term relationship. For example, if you surround yourself with individuals who believe they can not achieve their dreams, you will likely be influenced by their negative thinking and not take steps to achieve your own dreams. Mark Twain stated, "Keep away from people who try to belittle your ambitions. Small people always do that, but the really great make you feel that you, too, can become great." Godly relationships are with people who will encourage your better behaviour and help you on your healing journey. For example, if you are struggling with anger and you need healing in this area, associating with other angry people will hinder your progress to be free of anger. Scripture encourages perfume and incense, as it brings joy to the heart and the pleasantness of one's friend springs from his earnest counsel. Proverbs 27:9

Trust is a pillar:
Godly relationships require that you can confide in the other person without fear of betrayal. Hebrews 13:5 speaks about God's promise to never leave or forsake us. Are you in relationships where you feel secure and trust that the other person will not forsake you?

Create the habit of happiness:
Dr. Les & Dr. Leslie Parrott, authors of, <u>Saving Your Second Marriage Before It Starts</u> (2001), encourages people in relationships to create the habit of happiness. While these Christian authors speak mainly on marriage, their principles of cultivating the habit of happiness are important in all godly relationships. Dr. Les & Dr. Leslie Parrott make the following recommendations:

a) Relationships require people to maintain a positive attitude, even when things are going wrong. Dr. Les & Dr. Leslie Parrott state, "The negative person defends his attitudes with the rational of being realistic, while the positive person looks beyond the current state of affairs and sees people and situations in terms of possibilities."
b) Avoid the blame game. The couple suggests that individuals in relationships need to take responsibility for their own problems and overcome difficult situations.
c) Dr. Les & Dr. Leslie Parrott say that people can miss out on happiness because of self-pity. If self-pity is allowed to grow, it can drain the joy out of a relationship.

Have a love for people:
Love towards others is paramount in godly relationships. Jesus spoke about quality of friendships before he was crucified. In John 17:11, Jesus said, "I will remain in the world no longer, but they are still

in the world, and I am coming to you. Holy Father, protect them by the power of your name, the name you gave me, so that they may be one as we are one." Jesus described godly relationships to be one of unity and harmony. A relationship that is divided will not stand. In John 15:12, Jesus says, "This is my commandment, that you love one another as I have loved you. Greater love has no one than this, than to lay down one's life for his friends." In this verse, Jesus commands us to love others. Love repeatedly offers grace and forgiveness to others.

Free of Codependency:

How much effort do you exert to change the other person? Do you help others to the point of exhaustion until your own identity is lost? In her book, *Codependent No More,* Melanie Beattie (2008) defines a codependent as someone who has let another person's behaviour affect him or her, and who is obsessed with controlling that person's behaviour. Essentially, the codependent person believes that they will be happy if the other person changes. Are you codependent? Let's look at some basic principles around this topic.

- Codependent people get involved in relationships where people are unreliable, emotionally cold, needy and/or emotionally unavailable

- Codependent people try to control everything in the relationship without taking care of their own needs or desires

- Codependent people have trouble saying no when asked to volunteer, attend an event, take on additional projects at work or help other people. They give all of their time, emotions, finances, and other resources as a way to control others

- They have a strong desire to rescue other people because they believe they are doing what is best for that person

- Codependent people try to prevent people from experiencing hardships or consequences of their behaviour. In Matthew 16:21-28, scripture tells us when Peter learned that Jesus was going to suffer at the hands of Satan. Peter took Jesus aside and rebuked him. In Verse 22, Peter says, "Never, Lord! This shall never happen to you!" Jesus turned and said to Peter, "Get behind me, Satan! You are a stumbling block to me; you do not have in mind the things of God, but the things of men." Out of Peter's great love for Jesus, he was trying to protect Jesus from harm. However, if Peter had been successful, he would have interfered with God's perfect plan for salvation where Jesus took the penalty for the sins of the world, so that we can now accept Jesus as personal Savior and Lord. If Peter was successful, then Satan would have continued perpetuating evil and there would be no way for God's children to reconcile themselves to God. Codependent people try to protect other people from experiencing the natural consequences of their behaviour, just like Peter.

- Codependent people have a tendency to get involved in unhealthy or toxic relationships. They can be controlled by others, because they do not have clear, well-established boundaries. They strive for acceptance in unhealthy relationships because they think that if they can be good enough, or loving enough, they can change the other person's behaviour. Godly relationships require that all parties in the relationship benefit from the relationship. The nature of the relationship supports the independent identities within the relationship. Godly relationships require interdependence.

Relationships are free of violence:

Godly relationships are free of fear and violence. Is your relationship safe? Unhealthy relationships can be harmful to you and those around you. Have you considered whether or not your relationship is safe? According to Neighbors, Friends & Family Program (June 2006), there are some warning signs of Women's Abuse in relationships. These warning signs speak to women abused in heterosexual relationships.

WARNING SIGNS:

He puts her down.	She may be apologetic and make excuses for his behavior or become aggressive and angry.
He does all the talking and dominates the conversation.	She is nervous about talking when he's there.
He tries to suggest he is the victim and acts depressed.	She seems to be sick more often and misses work.
He tries to keep her away from you (other people).	She tries to cover her bruises.
He acts as if he owns her.	She makes excuses at the last minute about why she can't meet you or she tries to avoid you on the street.
He lies to make himself look good or exaggerates his good qualities.	She seems sad, lonely, withdrawn and afraid.
He acts like he is superior and of more value than others in his home.	She uses more drugs or alcohol to cope.

If you are in a violent relationship, contact your local police department and/or your local women's shelter for support and safety planning. For additional information on woman abuse and High Risk Signs visit this website http://www.neighboursfriendsandfamilies.ca/index.php.

Many survivors struggle with anger and may display behaviour that is abusive. Here is a list of behaviour that may be considered abusive. If you have any of these behaviours, it is possible to change them. Healing from the impact of childhood sexual abuse has helped survivors to significantly reduce and eliminate abusive behaviour.

Checklist: Am I behaving abusively?

- Do you tell your partner who your partner can talk to or socialize with?

- Do you call your partner names, criticize or embarrass your partner in front of others?

- Do you force or pressure your partner into doing something your partner doesn't want to do?

- Do you make your partner feel guilty to make the person do what you want them to do?

- Do you sabotage your partner's success?

- Do you follow your partner when the person is not with you?

- Do you constantly check up on your partner, such as listen to phone calls, check calls made or received on cell phone, call them constantly and get angry when they don't respond immediately?

- Do you check the mileage on your partner's car, do you frequently accuse your partner of cheating on you?

- Do you constantly blame your partner for everything?

- Do you have an explosive temper? Do you hit, punch, push or prevent your partner from leaving?

- Do you force your partner to have sex or engage in sexual practices that your partner is not comfortable with?

- Do you damage your partner's belongings, home, or throw things when angry?

- Do you threaten to harm your partner or others?

- Do you force your partner to use drugs or alcohol?

If you need support to change your behaviours, talk to a counseling professional in your community for additional support. It may also be beneficial to engage in couples counseling to help both of you heal. This is not an exhaustive list, but will help you to begin to evaluate your behaviour.

Healthy Boundaries:

Often, survivors who are raised in dysfunctional families struggle to create healthy boundaries. Dysfunctional families may display some of the following characteristics:

• lack of respect for other people's feelings, bodies and needs

• react to stress by retreating within themselves and close themselves off to the world

• keep their problems to themselves and reject any kind of support from others, especially professionals

• constantly complain about their problems, but do little to resolve their situation

• there are no clear boundaries in the parent-child relationship, role reversal is a major stressor on the relationship

• poor communication or no communication between family members

• family members blame each other for their problems and often lash out at each other

• family members do not support each other to solve their problems

• family members do not celebrate each other at birthdays, important events such as baptism, Christmas, academic success, school events

• they don't cope well with life stressors, nor deal with stress in a healthy way

• hold irrational or extreme beliefs

• they tend to make excuse for substance abuse or ignore that substance abuse is present in the family

• they do not respect authority figures such as teachers, police, church leadership

• families have high conflict with each other and others in the community

• family members do not take responsibility for their own actions or behaviours

• they often speak to each other harshly and with criticism

• they do not have boundaries regarding appropriate sexual behaviours

Survivors raised in dysfunctional families have little or no experience with healthy boundaries within the family. They often experience healthy boundaries in their relationships with others outside the family such as teachers, doctors and neighbors. Survivors raised in a dysfunctional home environment often have low self-esteem and lack self-confidence. To develop a healthy interaction pattern with others, it is imperative that survivors take steps to improve their self-esteem. Healthy boundaries require that you have an understanding of where to begin and end in your interaction with others. Learning to establish healthy boundaries is a necessary component for recovering survivors of childhood sexual abuse. Survivors can learn healthy boundaries by developing skills in assertive communication, learn to take care of themselves within relationships, learn to identify and respect other people's right and needs, learn to give voice to their own wants and desires and respecting the voice of others.

Healthy boundaries are both physical and emotional. Physical boundaries define who can touch you, how others can touch you and where they can touch your body. Physical boundaries require that you respect the same with others. Emotional boundaries recognize and accept your uniqueness of emotions and require that you manage your emotions and permit others to do the same. In addition, emotional boundaries ensure that you do not feel overly responsible for the feelings and needs of others, while neglecting your own. For instance, if you become upset because others around you are upset, then you do not have healthy emotional boundaries.

Healthy boundaries define how you interact with others and how you give permission for others to interact with you. Survivors of childhood sexual abuse have had their physical and emotional boundaries violated. Thus, it is important to understand that at an early age you learned how to interact with others without boundaries. You learned that others can touch you in anyway they want, do whatever they want to your body and possessions, and treat you in anyway the abuser desires. If you lived in a dysfunctional family, you may have learned to interact with others without boundaries leading to your life being filled with chaos and chronic stress.

Healthy boundaries are not rigid or loosely defined. Rigid boundaries lead to you closing yourself from other people. You can present yourself as emotional distant, meaning not sharing or showing your emotions. You don't let anyone into your life! There is always an invisible wall to protect you from a perceived threat. You keep the wall between you and others, so no one can get over or though, which prevents others from getting to know you personally and stops them from seeing your authentic self. Loosely defined boundaries may present you as saying yes to someone when you want to say no; you may be sexually promiscuous; expect others to read your mind instead of expressing your opinion and feelings; and you may jump into a sexual relationship with someone before assessing if this person is right for you and so forth.

Healthy boundaries are firm yet flexible. Healthy boundaries permit a separate togetherness in your relationship with others. You are able to negotiate and compromise without loosing your internal sense of personal identity. When you have healthy boundaries you are comfortable with yourself and are able to make others comfortable in your presence. For example, you do not criticize others to make yourself feel good or look confident!

MODULEFOUR
Emotions

Managing Your Emotions

CHAPTER TWENTY

Understanding Your Emotions

THIS MODULE WILL HELP YOU ACCURATELY IDENTIFY YOUR FEELINGS AND THE LEVELS OF INTENSITY OF your feelings. It will also help you to recognize your body sensations that contribute to your thoughts and behaviour. The most common labels used for feelings are sad, angry, mad, lonely and happy. Survivors have a spectrum of emotions and each emotion will have a different degree of intensity depending on the situation or event. Body sensations are also felt when we experience various emotions. These body sensations can vary in intensity. For example, if you are really angry, you may feel a hot sensation on your face. You may be so nervous concerning meeting someone that you might be "weak in the knees." Your body sensations and feelings can give you important information about the way you are thinking and the way you are behaving in a given situation. To manage your emotions, it is important to identify your feelings and body sensations.

Here is a list of body sensations. Do you experience any body sensations? Below, put a cross at the body sensation you experience. Are there other body sensations you experience?

- heart palpitations
- tingling in fingers
- nausea
- lump in throat
- numbness in body
- clarity
- lightheadedness

- pressure or heaviness
- butterflies in stomach
- knot in stomach
- blurred or distorted vision
- sweating
- clear visions
- feeling of swaying

- tightness in chest
- sensation of warmth or cold
- spacious and expansive
- glowing
- bubbly or giggly inside
- others _____

Now, take a moment and list the various emotions that you have experienced. Do you experience one or two emotions more than other emotions? Complete the sentences below:

YOU ARE A MIRACLE

I sometimes feel_____

I often feel_____

I mostly feel_____

I never feel_____

Take a moment and review the various feelings identified in this chart. Are there other feelings you can add?

FEELING CHART

Abandoned	Sneaky	Hurt	Eager	Capable
Defeated	Miserable	Honored	Sympathetic	Flustered
Grateful	Ignored	Panicky	Blissful	Free
Sexy	Inspired	Frightened	Pity	Frantic
Mysterious	Lustful	Fearful	Energetic	Childlike
Adequate	Lazy	Stupid	Restless	Troubled
Delighted	Infatuated	Attractive	Refreshed	Violent
Naughty	Obsessed	Peaceful	Remorseful	Unsettled
Shocked	Anxious	Mean	Isolated	Deceitful
Greedy	Discontent	Kind	Rejected	Blissful
Nervous	Spiteful	Petrified	Relieved	Competitive
Sneaky	Helpful	Loved	Ecstatic	Tense
Jealous	Startled	Jumpy	Sad	Generous
Affectionate	Apathetic	Melancholy	Flustered	Tired
despair	Helpless	Loving	Empty	Terrified
Grief	Sorrow	Pleased	Relaxed	Apologetic
Silly	Distraught	Proud	Scared	Curious
Skeptical	Awed	Lonely	Happy	Exasperated
Guilty	Confused	Precarious	Righteous	Trapped
Agony	Overwhelmed	Joyous	Bored	Troubled
Gullible	Awkward	Mad	Settled	Envious
Solemn	Disturbed	Intimidated	Calm	Aggressive
Angry	Excited	Rage	Weepy	Arrogant
Ambivalent	Hate	Betrayed	Vulnerable	Shy

Your
EMOTIONS

To help you identify your emotions, write down two experiences or situations (not related to your abuse) that have happened to you in the past two weeks. Use space below to record each situation you experienced in the past two weeks. Using the Feeling Chart & Body Sensation List, circle the emotions and body sensations that you have experienced. Next to each item you circled, rate the intensity of the emotion from the least intense (10%) to the most intense (100%). When rating your emotions in terms of intensity, think of a thermometer. Which emotion did you experience most intensely? Which emotion did you experience that was the least intense? Your emotions have a direct influence on your thoughts and your behaviour. It's important to identify how you are feeling (including body sensations) to determine what thoughts are created from them and what behaviour you can use to cope with your emotions.

Situation 1: Explain your situation in the space provided.

_____
_____
_____
_____
_____
_____
_____

Situation 2: Explain your situation in the space provided.

_____
_____
_____
_____
_____
_____
_____

Freedom From Guilt & Shame

Most survivors feel guilt and shame, due to the abuse that they experienced. The Responsibility Pie Technique adapted from Greenberger & Padesky (1995), is another strategy to help you identify and externalize your feelings of guilt and shame that caused a low mood. This technique allows you to identify all the contributing factors and persons responsible for your feelings of guilt and shame. Many survivors believe they own 100% of the blame and guilt for the sexual abuse. It is important that you move away from that false belief. Each Responsibility Pie chart will differ for each survivor. Guilt and shame can be negative factors that hinder your healing. Going through a process of identifying what other factors, individuals or systems that may be responsible in the situation will allow you to appropriately place the blame where it belongs and absolve you of some or all of the responsibility. The aim of the responsibility pie is to use the guilt to motivate you to take another step of faith in your healing journey. The responsibility pie provides an additional benefit that will allow you the opportunity to talk about tough topics such as spiritual confusion. This is a powerful tool that gives you permission to discuss difficult questions about your relationship with God and other spiritual matters. For example, if a woman's pie identifies that she blames God for 100% of the abuse, then the woman may need additional education and support to see that the original sin, caused by the devil, not God, has contributed to your current circumstances. She may also need more counseling to help her work out feelings of anger she may have towards God.

While the pie chart is to help externalize your guilt and blame, it can have additional benefits to help springboard you to another level of healing. Remember, God tells you in Hebrews 10:17, that He forgets your sin, once you confess it to Him. Often survivors feel guilt and shame because they believe they have done something to encourage the sexual abuse. My prayer is that this activity will give you a greater understanding of why you are holding onto guilt and shame. While the responsibility pie will focus on removing full blame from you, the survivor, it's an excellent opportunity for pastors, therapist or counseling professional to further assess where you are spiritually. Two major challenges that hinder survivors' spiritual growth are spiritual confusion and lack of scriptural truth. You may need a pastor, social worker or professional counselor to help you work through the challenges or obstacles that are impeding your ability to receive God's love.

SAMPLE OF RESPONSIBILITY
PIES OF TAMAR'S STORY

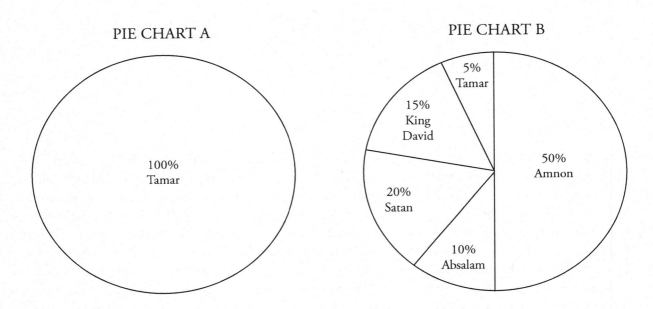

PIE CHART A

100%
Tamar

PIE CHART B

5%
Tamar

15%
King
David

50%
Amnon

20%
Satan

10%
Absalam

Previously on page 21, we learned about Tamar's experience of sexual abuse. Using Tamar's story as an example she could have two different Responsibility Pie Charts. The Responsibility Pie Chart A highlights that she fully blamed herself for the sexual abuse. After asking her a series of questions and identify other parties or influences that may have attributed to the abuse, Tamar's pie chart changes significantly (Pie Chart B). Most importantly in Pie Chart B her self blame decreases because place accountability and blame on the appropriate person, Amnon. Review Pie Chart A & Chart B above.

Responsibility Pie
WORKSHEET

(Adapted from Mind Over Mood by Greenberger & Padesky.1995. The Guilford Press)

1. Answer the following questions to reflect on your personal situation:

How much did I contribute to the problem?
How much did others contribute to the problem?
How much did other unpredictable factors or events contribute to the situation?
Does my spirituality contribute to the situation? How much?
Does the original sin between Adam & Eve affect this situation? How much?
Is Satan responsible or contributing to my problem? How much?
Is God responsible or contributing to my problem? How much?

2. Draw a circle. Divide into sections that resemble a pie and fill in who is responsible. Total responsibility is 100 %.

3. How much did you rate God's involvement in your situation? How much did you rate Satan's involvement in your situation? How does this responsibility pie chart affect your feelings of guilt and shame? Does this pie identify spiritual questions or scriptural truths you want to explore further? If so, please describe.

_____
_____
_____
_____
_____
_____
_____
_____

4. How is Satan using sexual abuse to steal from you? List the ways in which Satan is using sexual abuse to steal/take from you? For example, a survivor blamed her mother for years for the sexual abuse toward her by her mother's boyfriend. This survivor identified that Satan took from her a loving relationship with her mother.

_____
_____
_____
_____
_____
_____
_____
_____

5. Do you see God as 100 % or responsible in any way? If so, write in the space below exactly how God is responsible.

_____
_____
_____
_____
_____
_____
_____
_____

Dealing With Guilt and Shame

Sexual abuse can create fertile ground for the spiritual struggles to develop. Murray-Swank (2005) quotes Murray-Swank (2004) who reports that childhood sexual abuse survivors often experience a sense of spiritual disconnection and isolation, anger at God, and feelings of abandonment by God. Murray-Swank (2005) quotes Exline et al., (2000) who report survivors experience anger towards God and alienation from God has been associated with increased depression and anxiety. It is normal for survivors to ask God where are you? According to scripture, Satan is 100% responsible for causing the trauma of sexual abuse you endured. Jesus warns us in the scripture about Satan, John 10:10-11 states, "The thief (Satan) comes only to steal and kill and destroy; I have come that they may have life, and have it to the full." This scripture tells us that God is the life-giver and comes to earth so that we can live abundantly. It is Satan who comes to destroy you. Sexual abuse is the tool of Satan, to ignite war against God's children - including you. Satan uses sexual abuse to destroy your life and keep you from having a relationship with God. God often gets blamed for things such as natural disasters and for childhood sexual abuse. Satan does everything he can to keep you from everything that is good that comes from God. The responsibility pie activity would also show you that you are not responsible for the abuse you experienced. Often survivors believe that they did something to cause the perpetrator to abuse them. For example, a young girl who was sexually abused by her foster father was sexually abused from the age of 5 to 18 years. Over the years the abuse escalated from molestation to sexual assault by the age of 10. She blamed herself for being sexually assaulted until she was thirty-six years old. She carried the blame for more than 20 years. She believed that if she kicked while her perpetrator was raping her, she would have been able to stop him. She carried the blame until she was able to recognize that her body size was quite small compared to that of an adult male body who was holding her down. His weight was so heavy that she also struggled to breathe. When she understood that she physically had no physical power to stop the abuse, she was able to relinquish her self blame and place it where it belonged on the perpetrator. Understanding sexual abuse was a form of the spiritual warfare, as she removed the blame from God and herself and rightfully placed it appropriately on Satan.

It is okay to acknowledge that you blame God, but it is vital that you ask God to help you work through it. God has extended his hand of grace to you and he is not angry that you see him responsible for the trauma you experienced. He loves you just as you are. He loves you so much he wants to set you free from the troubles that plaque you because of the sexual abuse. As you increase in your faith and continue to grow spiritually, you will begin to see God's love for you and his hand in your life. 1 John 4: 9-10 states, "This is how much God showed his love among for us: He sent his one and only Son into the world that we might live through him. This is love: not that we loved God, but that he loved us and sent his Son as an atoning sacrifice our sins." God's love is further described in 1 John 4:15-19, "If anyone acknowledges that Jesus is the Son of God, God lives in *her* and *she* in God. And so we know and rely on the love God has for us. God is love. Whoever lives in love lives in God, and God in *her* (italic is my emphasis). In this way, love is made complete among us so that we can have confidence on the day of judgment, because in this world we are like Him. There is no fear in love. But perfect love drives out fear, because fear has to do with punishment. The one who fears is not made perfect in love. We love because he first loved us." This

111

scripture can be hard for survivors to understand. To change this way of thinking is challenging but not impossible. Jesus is an example of a life that lived and breathed love for you.

Forgiveness Is a Gift to You

What does forgiveness mean to you? Forgiveness is something every survivors grapples with on their healing journey. When people think of forgiveness they think of forgiveness as a reconciliation event. An event that once completed, is resolved. Forgiveness is much more than an event, it is a process. Forgiveness is a choice. It is a daily decision to let go of resentment, anger, fear, bitterness and hurt. Forgiveness does not mean that you deny your abusers' responsibility for hurting you, nor does forgiveness minimize or justify the abuse you endured. Forgiveness is necessary to improve your quality of life. Forgiveness can make way for you to develop compassion for yourself and other people. Forgiveness can lead to healthy relationships, greater spiritual intimacy with God, psychological well being, reduced substance abuse, significantly reduced depression and anxiety, reduce stress and other psychological distress. Forgiveness is something that God speaks about in the Bible. God calls sinners to seek him and promises to forgive them. It is because of forgiveness that Jesus Christ came to earth to die for mankind. Forgiveness is necessary to be able to enjoy life. Forgiveness sets you free from past mistakes and wrongs done to you and by you. It will give you hope for the future.

Matthew 18: 21-35 highlights that God sees unforgiveness as unacceptable and tells how often survivors should forgive. Easier said than done right? …absolutely!! There are times in a survivor's life when she is unable to forgive her abuser because of the deep hurt inflicted by the trauma of sexual abuse. She may also struggle to forgive those who "let" the abuse occur in the first place. She may struggle to forgive people who did not intervene to stop the abuse and/or denied the abuse occurred in the first place. Scripture tells us that God calls survivors to forgive their perpetrator and others who have hurt them. Forgiveness does not mean having a personal relationship with your abuser. Forgiveness only requires you to protect yourself from further harm and ensure you have healthy boundaries in place.

Survivors expend a lot of energy in keeping their angers, hurts and fears pushed down.

John Arnott, author of What Christians Should Know About the Importance of Forgiveness Series (1997) tells us holding on to hurts and judgments is a luxury you and I can't afford. It is like giving Satan a key to your house. John Arnott says "we are to give others a gift they don't deserve when there is no question that you have been sinned against, hurt and violated by them. He states there is an outstanding debt that person owe us, but we can give them an undeserving gift—Forgiveness. Arnott challenges people to take a step into the mercy of God as to say, "I want mercy to triumph over justice" because this is what God is asking us for. When we extend the hand of forgiveness you are saying that the grace of God is more than enough for you. Arnott (1997) suggests that the only place Satan cannot follow and accuse. That place is in the grace of Jesus Christ which is the place of mercy, love and forgiveness. If we live in grace and mercy, Satan cannot follow you there and he has no rights to you there. As you live in mercy and grace, releasing forgiveness to yourself and others you will find amazing freedom.

What do you do when your heart is like a stone and you are unable to forgive?

If you are struggling to forgive, ask God each day to change your heart. Simply saying this prayer every day will soften your heart over time and help you to make the choice to forgive. You will be able to forgive when the time is right for you.

Here is a sample prayer that you may pray at this time. You may wish to personalize it to fit your situation.

> *"Lord I am unable to forgive right now because the pain is so great. Help me to be free from the pain and shame of sexual abuse. Lord, help me to change my heart so I can be free of the bitterness and hatred. Lord, I know forgiveness means to have boundaries and you do not require me to have a relationship with my abuser or others who have hurt me. Lord help me to extend the hand of forgiveness so that I can be set free from my anger, hurts and fear. Help me to be compassionate toward myself. Lord, help me to be an instrument of peace in Jesus' name. Amen."*

I recommend that you read John Arnott's book, *What Christians Should Know About the Importance of Forgiveness* (1997).

Spiritual Affirmations

A SPIRITUAL AFFIRMATION IS AN ACTION OR A PROCESS OF AFFIRMING WHO YOU ARE AS A CHILD OF GOD. An affirmation can be a formal declaration about yourself and your relationship with God. It is your inner dialogue and the words you speak about yourself that affirm your positive attributes and character. They reflect your life experiences, your beauty, your accomplishments and successes. An affirmation needs to speak of how God sees you. The statement is free of guilt, blame, negative thoughts, behaviour, and attitudes. It is a declaration to honor everything about you and the progress you made in healing. Affirmations are to focus solely on you and no one else. Spiritual affirmations give God permission to operate in your life. They will keep your mind focused on the presence of God and tap into the power of God to manifest whatever you desire to be affirmed about you. Affirmations are words spoken in faith. These positive statements, when spoken in the Name of Jesus, will permit the incredible power of God to help you overcome insurmountable obstacles. It is a powerful tool to change your emotional state.

Affirmations can be about any topic such as abundance and prosperity, mental health, forgiveness, physical healing, love, self-confidence, weight loss, or a healthy lifestyle. The list of topics for your affirmations is endless. Whatever topic you choose, it should focus on your spiritual growth in that area. Your personal declarations serve to empower you during difficult times or struggles as a constant reminder of your inseparable relationship with God. An affirmation is an uplifting message you tell yourself that is grounded in God's truth and His Word.

Are you ready to write your own affirmation? This is a really fun and simple activity. Here's an example of an affirmation for you to look at, which I hope will help you to get started. This affirmation was written by a woman who was sexually abused as a child. Her affirmation was to affirm the presence of God in her life and the security she felt being His daughter.

Example: Self-affirmation

"God's peace eases the pain. The Holy Spirit whispers a message of love and understanding that is embraced in every part of my being. My body responds with its own message of love, life and healing. I am filled with peace and I'm grateful to God for His precious gift of peace. I find this peace whenever I want to experience it and rely on it. I am at peace with God. I am my own person, a precious child of God. I was made in His image of goodness. I am a mirror of God's glory. I can decide for myself what appropriate behaviour is for me now and what fits with the loving person that I am. I know from my own experiences that it is okay to ask God for help when I feel confused, scared, tired or doubt myself. I can call on God to help me when I'm worried about my physical, emotional and mental health. I can ask God for help when I'm feeling hurt or unclear about something. Knowing and trusting God as I do, I can appreciate His truth, honesty and purity. I am free from the rules and expectations of others. I don't need to please anyone. I have learned that God is love and forgiveness. God understands my mistakes and does not expect me to be perfect. God understands my humanness, my weakness and is not there to criticize me. Rather, God wants me to live a life of love and forgiveness. He gave me His Son Jesus, who set an example of love and forgiveness by His own life. I was the only one there the night Jesus found me and wrapped His loving arms around me. In my safe place, I can rest in the security of that moment. There is nothing in the world strong enough to take away what God has given me. He has given me joy. The joy of the Lord is my strength. Joy that the world did not give to me nor can this world take away. My divine heritage is freedom; freedom to be what God created me to be. Freedom to do what I know in my heart is the right thing to do. I can let go of doubt and fear and stand firm in my belief that with God—anything is possible, from making minor changes in my routine to breaking free from negative beliefs and habits. As I stand with God, I claim my spiritual freedom. God's love is a powerful presence that I can hold onto through my most difficult times. I know that God is always there, giving me strength in times of trouble, and He carries me when I need to be carried. I know that regardless of what life brings me, with God, I will never face them alone!"

Creating an affirmation:

There are several strategies to help you create an affirmation. Here are some suggestions to help you create your own affirmation. If you want your circumstances in your life to change, you need to make a commitment to apply your affirmation to your life by reading it aloud every day.

1. Take 10 minutes to interview someone you trust and respect who knows you intimately. The purpose of interviewing is to highlight your positive attributes, character, as well as highlight your successes and accomplishments. The answers to the interview questions below can then be used to help you create an affirmation. You can also add your own interview questions, but they must be positive reflections about you.

Here are some suggested questions you can ask someone:
   a) What wonderful things do you see in me?

    b) What are my strengths?

    c) In what areas have you seen me succeed?

    d) What do you appreciate about me?

    e) In what ways have you seen God bless me?

    f) How have I blessed others?

2. Complete the following statements about yourself to create an affirmation. You may also organize these sentences into a poem or story to create your affirmation.

I hold the power within me to_____

I am able to _____

I am free from_____

I always reach out with love to _____

I let go of_____ and I accept God's truth about me.

I accept the love of_____ so that I can be_____

I embrace _____

In my body I feel _____

God's presence is _____

I am a participant of life who_____

I have a lot of love to give to_____

I am loving toward _____

I seek God's heart to _____

I nurture hope, peace, joy within myself so that I may _____

God's blessings are _____

I trust in God's love at all times even when I am _____

My eyes see the beauty of _____

God guides all of my steps so that I can confidently _____

I choose to love_____

I am the heart of Christ when I_____

I trust completely in God's infinite wisdom and His deep love for me so_____

God is ever present in my life. Nothing can separate me from God. I am secure to_____

God sends his angels to _____

3. Another way to create a spiritual affirmation is to use the book of Psalms in the Bible. There are 150 psalms to encourage you and help deepen your relationship with God. There are many different genres of psalms. The book of Psalms brings comfort to people who are facing problems. The psalmist requests help from God to intervene in his situations. The book of psalms is helpful when writing affirmations because the psalmist expresses his pain to God, affirms his trust in God,

affirms God's character and His presence in his life. When you speak the Psalms, you are coming into agreement with God, and His power is immediately released to answer your prayers, remove obstacles in your life, and increase your spirituality. I recommend Psalm 27, Psalm 37, Psalm 121 and Psalm 139 in the New International Version Bible to help you create your affirmation.

4. There are hundreds of published daily devotionals, daily prayers, spiritual affirmations, inspirational material and lyrics from your favorite songs on the market that you can use to help create your own positive affirmation. I recommend the following books:

Iyanla Vanzant's book called, *Don't Give It Away: A Workbook of Self-Awareness and Self-Affirmations for Young Women. (1999).*

John Bevere's book called, *Drawing Near: A Life of Intimacy with God. (2004).*

Toni Sortor & Pamela McQuade's book called, *365 Daily Devotionals For Couples: Inspiration for the marriage you've always wanted.(2007).*

Joyce Meyer's book called, *Starting Your Day Right: Devotions for each Morning of the Year. (2003).*

Atmosphere for Miracles

In traditional trauma-focused therapies, trauma survivors are encouraged to retell their story in the form of a trauma narrative. A trauma narrative can be done in many forms such as a collage of pictures, poetry and telling the story of abusive incidents. While traditional strategies are helpful they require professional support. Disclosure is done over a period of time to help survivors make sense of their experiences.

Instead of creating a trauma narrative, I believe giving daily, positive testimonies will help survivors focus on their personal growth and healing successes. It gives God glory when you give a detailed account of how a relationship with God has transformed your life by His power. It is an opportunity to create an atmosphere for miracles, in your life and for others. A testimony does not focus on traumatic thoughts but is a coping strategy to help organize your emotions and healing into a more manageable and understandable story. God commands you to share your testimony to express all He has done in your life. A testimony is a public confession of your love for God. It overcomes Satan and helps you grow in your faith. Your original testimony can be spoken or written, shared with others or your own private declaration. As you grow in your faith, God will give you the boldness to share your testimony with others. In Acts 4:29-31, Peter and John prayed "Now, Lord, consider their threats and enable your servants to speak your word with great boldness. Stretch out your hand to heal and perform miraculous signs and wonders through the name of your holy servant Jesus." After they prayed, the place where they were meeting was shaken. And they were all filled with the Holy Spirit and spoke the word of God boldly.

Creating an atmosphere for miracles to occur, involves giving frequent, shorter testimony throughout your day, giving God praise and thanks for what He is doing in your life every moment. This shorter, daily testifying is for you only. As you become more confident in sharing how God has changed your life, you may want to share your testimony with others. Testifying can be fun and an opportunity to express the joy that is within you! Testifying involves a desire to speak your testimony using your own expression and personality style. Speaking aloud to yourself about your positive life experiences and encounters with Christ confirms how your life has changed. Testifying allows you to bear witness and focus on the reason why you changed and your commitment to Christ. Testifying consistently involves sharing real and relevant life issues and will help remind you what Christ is doing in your life. You can testify about anything you want such as God's gifts He's given you, His faithfulness, grace, goodness and mercy, challenges which God helped you to overcome, success and accomplishments that were achieved, His love and the healing He has done in your life.

Below are some statements you can use to help you give short, quick testimonies to create an atmosphere of miracles!

1. God truly blessed me this week when_____. God is _____. All Glory and Honor go to Him for what He has done and continues to do!

2. Today I was _____but God removed the obstacle _____that was in my way. I am no longer_____.

3. Praise the Lord for the wonderful news you received about_____.

4. Thank God! He does not give up on me because my breakthrough is almost here!

5. I am tremendously blessed because of what the Lord did today. Today the Lord_____.

6. Jesus, thank You that you have already won the battle. This challenging situation, _____ is not mine to struggle with alone. The battle is not mine, it's the Lord's.

7. Lord, thank you for giving me the desires of my heart. Today, the Lord helped me to _____.

8. My good days outweigh my bad days. I am healed. I am no longer depressed [fill in the blank].

Self-Care Plan

So far you have learned a lot about how your thoughts and behaviour impact your mood. Now we need to pull all that you learned together to develop a self-care plan. A self-care plan identifies your emotions, the intensity of the emotions and the various strategies you are using to take care of yourself. As you have learned, your thoughts influence your behaviour and in turn they influence your emotions and vise versa, depending on the direction of your Trauma Focused-Cognitive Behaviour Therapy cycle. Where you are on the Trauma Focused-Cognitive Behaviour Therapy cycle will determine what strategy you will use to take care of yourself and help you on your healing journey such as visualization, exercise, expressing your emotions, soaking in the presence of God, prayer or testifying. Self care plans are most effective when you get into a routine and use the strategies every day. Using the strategies you learned consistently for the next 30 days will help to be habit forming. The more you use the strategies the more comfortable you will become using them.

It is also necessary you take steps to maintain your physical health in addition to your mental health. Do you exercise regularly and eat healthy? I would encourage you to work with a dietician to help you with developing a healthy eating lifestyle. A dietician can help you with learning how to read nutrition labels, learning healthy food portions and other services to help you maintain your health. Do you get enough sleep? If you are having difficulties with your sleep, it is important for you to talk with your doctor to explore and rule out any medical reasons for lack of sleep. Are you increasing your social support? It is important that you develop a support network, spend time with people you trust and engage in activities that make you laugh and enjoy yourself such as a sport or hobby.

Spiritual Self-Care
ACTIVITY

Over the next week log your emotions and rate their intensity from a scale of least intense (10%) to most intense (100%). After you rate your emotion, write down what strategy you will use to help take care of yourself. To take care of yourself, you may use cognitive strategies from Module two, a behaviour strategy from Module three and/or emotion regulation strategies from Module four. Use the Spiritual Self Care Chart on page 123 to help you organize your work.

SPIRITUAL SELF CARE PLAN

DATE & TIME	EMOTION (What are you feeling/ body sense?)	INTENSITY OF EMOTION (Rate intensity from 10% - 100%)	COGNITIVE COPING TECHNIQUE (Module 2)	BEHAVIORAL COPING STRATEGY (Module 3)	EMOTIONAL COGNITIVE STRATEGY (Module 4)
MON.	Fear because of frequent night-mares, Increased heart rate.	75%	Change my dream —invite God into my dream	Soaking in the presence of God	Responsibility Pie Chart
TUES.					
WED.					
THURS.					
FRI.					
SAT.					
SUN.					

WRAPPING UP!

My heart's desire is that this book encourages you on your healing journey. God has an exciting purpose and destiny for your life. God's heart for you is for personal deliverance, revival, and reconciliation with Him. God's passion is to love you and heal the areas in your life that were touched by the sexual abuse you experienced. My prayer is that this book will release God's potential within you and unlock the desires within. My vision is to help women who have a desire to rise up from their situations that are keeping them in bondage and living a victorious life that God has ordained for them. May you grow in your faith and love and be inspired to follow God's predestined plan for your life. God declared that strength and dignity are your clothing! Your position in Him is strong and secure! My prayer is that you will have a miraculous encounter with your Heavenly Father as you embrace His love! You Are A Miracle!

In conclusion, let's have a look at the lyrics of this beautiful song, *He Knows My Name* by Tommy Walker. It speaks of how intimate God knows you and how deeply He loves you!

HE KNOWS MY NAME
I have a Maker
He formed my heart
Before even time began
My life was in his hands
Chorus:
He knows my name
He knows my every thought
He sees each tear that falls
And He hears me when I call
I have a Father
He calls me His own
He'll never leave me
No matter where I go
Chorus:
He knows my name
He knows my every thought
He sees each tear that falls
And He hears me when I call

Song by Tommy Walker

References

Bass, E., & Davis, L. (2008). Courage to Heal: A Guide for Women Survivors of Child Sexual Abuse. New York, Harper-Collins Publishers.

Beste, Jennifer. 2005. Recovery from Sexual Violence and Socially Mediated Dimensions of God's Grace: Implications for Christian communities. *SCE* 18(2):89-112.

Beattie, Melody. 1987. Codependent No More: How to Stop Controlling Others and Start Caring for Yourself. New York. Walker and Company.

Brennan, Shannon & Taylor-Butts, Andrea (December 2008). Sexual Assault in Canada: 2004-2007. Statistics Canada: Canadian Centre for Justice Statistics
Catalogue no. 85F0033M — No. 19 ISSN 1496-4562 ISBN 978-1-100-11163-6
http://www.statcan.gc.ca/pub/85f0033m2008019-eng.pdf

Burns, David. 1989. The Feeling Good Handbook. New York: Penguin.

Cheston, S., Piedmont, R., Eanes, B., and Lavin, P. (January 2003). Changes in clients' images of God over the course of outpatient therapy. *Counselling and Values.* 47:96-108.

Child Sexual Abuse. The Canadian Badgley Royal Commission, Report on Sexual Offences Against Children and Youths.1984. pg.175.

Cohen, J.A., Mannarino, A.P., Deblinger, E., & Berliner, L. (2009). Cognitive-behaviour therapy for children and adolescents. In E. B. Foa, T. M. Keane, M.J. Friedman, & J.A. Cohen (eds.), *Effective treatments for PTSD: Practice guidelines from the International Society for Traumatic Stress Studies* (pp. 223-244). New York, NY: Guildford Press.

Connora, P., and Higgins, D. November 2008. Case Report: The "HEALTH" model – Part 2: case study of a guideline-based treatment program for Complex PTSD relating to childhood sexual abuse. *Sexual and Relationship Therapy.* 23(4):401–410.

Department of Justice Canada 2011-04-26. http://www.justice.gc.ca/eng/pi/fv-vf/facts-info/child-enf.html

Dr. Les and Dr. Leslie Parrott. Saving your second marriage before it starts. Nine questions to ask before and after you marry. Michigan, Zondervan. 2001. ISBN:031 0260957.

Dull.V.T. and Skokan, L.A.1995. A cognitive model of religion's influence on health. *Journal of Social Issues.* 54(2):49-64.

Family Violence in Canada: A Statistical Profile 2007. Canadian Centre for Justice Statistics. Catalogue No. 85-224-XIE, ISSN 1480-7165. Ottawa, Ontario, Canada.

Fleming, Jon, MD in association with the MediResource Clinical Team. The Nine Rules of Sleep Hygiene. (2011). http://chealth.canoe.ca/channel_section_details.asp?text_id=1115&channel_id=135&relation_id2779

Fouque, P. and Glachan, M. 2000. The Impact of Christian Counselling on Survivors of Sexual Abuse. *Counselling Psychology Quarterly,* 13(2): 201- 220.

Frost, Jack. *Spiritual Slavery to Spiritual Sonship: Your Destiny Awaits You.* Shippenburg, Destiny Image Publishers. 2006. ISBN: 10: 0-7684-2385-6

Gail, Terry Lynn. (July 2006). Spirituality and coping with life stress among survivors of childhood sexual abuse. *Child Abuse & Neglect.* 30(7):829-844.

Gall, T., Basque, V., Damasceno-Scott, M., and Vardi, G. 2007.Spirituality and the Current Adjustment of Adult Survivors of Childhood Sexual Abuse. *Journal for the Scientific Study of Religion.* 46(1):101–111.

Ganje-Fling, M, McCarthy, P., Haijiang, K., & Houg, B. (January 2000). Effects of childhood sexual abuse on client spiritual well-being. *Counseling and Values.* 44(2):253-258.

Ganje-Fling, M.A. and P. McCarthy.1996. Impact of childhood sexual abuse on client spiritual development: Counselling implications. *Journal of Counseling and Development*.74:253-258.

Ganje-Fling, Marilyn A. & McCarthy, Patricia (Dec 2011). Impact of Childhood Sexual Abuse on Client Spiritual Development: Counseling Implications. *Journal of Counseling & Development*. Volume 74, Issue 3, Article first published online: 23 DEC 2011

Glaister, J.A., and E.Abel.2001.Experiences of women healing from child sexual abuse. *Archives of Psychiatric Nursing*.15(4):188-194.

Greenberger D., and Padesky, C. Mind Over Mood. New York: Guilford (1995).

Gubia, P., and Jacobs, R. March 2009. Exploring the impact on counsellors of working with spiritually abused clients. *Mental Health, Religion & Culture*. 12 (2):191–204.

Hall, T.A.1995. Spiritual effects of childhood sexual abuse in adult Christian Women. *Journal of Psychology and Theology*.23:129-34.

Health Canada Discussion papers on Health/Family Violence Issues: The impact of violence on Mental Health-A Guide to the literature. February 1995. ISBN: 0-66-23605-x

Kennedy, J.E., Davis, R.C., and Taylor, B.1998. Changes in spirituality and well-being among victims of sexual assault. *Journal for the Scientific Study of Religion*. 37(2):322-328.

Lemoncelli.J. and A.Carey. 1996. The psychospiritual dynamics of adult survivors of abuse. *Counselling and Values*. 40:175-84.

McDonagh, A., Friedman, M., McHugo, G., Ford, J., Sengupta, A., Mueser, K., Demment, C., Fournier, D., Schnurr, P., & Descamps, M. Randomized Trial of Cognitive-Behavioural Therapy for Chronic Posttraumatic Stress Disorder in Adult Female Survivors of Childhood Sexual Abuse. *Journal of Consulting and Clinical Psychology*, Vol 73(3), June 2005, 515-524

Murray-Swank, N. & Pargament, K.I God, where are you?: Evaluating a spiritually-integrated. Mental Health, Religion & Culture September 2005; 8(3): 191–203.

Paragament, K.I. 1997. The psychology of religion and coping. In Handbook of religion and mental health. Sand Diego: Academic Press.

Pargament, K. and Murray-Swank, N. 2005. God, where are you?: Evaluating a spiritually-integrated intervention for sexual abuse. *Mental Health, Religion & Culture.* September 2005; 8(3):191–203.

Pattison, Stephen. 1998. Suffer Little Children: The Challenge of Child Abuse and Neglect in Theology. *T&S.* 9:36-58.

Post, B., and Wade, N. 2009. Religion and Spirituality in Psychotherapy: A Practice-Friendly Review of Research. *Journal of Clinical Psychology: In Session*, Vol. 65(2), 131--146 (2009) & 2009 Wiley Periodicals, Inc. Published online in Wiley InterScience (www.interscience.wiley.com).

Public Health Agency of Canada, Canadian Incident Study of Reported Child Abuse and Neglect-2003 Major Findings. pg. 39.

Rudolfsson, L. and Tidefors, I. 2009. "Shepherd My Sheep": Clerical Readiness to Meet Psychological and Existential Needs from Victims of Sexual Abuse. *Pastoral Psychol.* 58:79–92.

Shea, D. 2008. Effects of Sexual Abuse by Catholic Priests on Adults Victimized as Children. *Sexual Addiction & Compulsivity.* 15:250–268. Copyright © Taylor & Francis Group, LLC. ISSN: 1072-0162 print / 1532-5318 online
DOI: 10.1080/10720160802288993

Snyder, Howard, N. (2000, July). *Sexual assault of young children as reported to law enforcement: victim, incident, and offender characteristics.* Retrieved from http://bjs.ojp.usdoj.gov/content/pub/pdf/saycrle.pdf

Snyder, C.R. and Heinze, L. S. 2005. Forgiveness as a mediator of the relationship between PTSD and hostility in survivors of childhood abuse. *Cognition and Emotion.*19(3): 413-431.

Statistics Canada. (July 2005). Family Violence in Canada: A Statistical Profile
Catalogue no. 85-224 http://www.statcan.gc.ca/pub/85-224-x/85-224-x2005000-eng.pdf

The Quest Study Bible. New International Version. 1984. Zondervan Publishing House. Grand Rapids, Michigan. ISBN: 0-310-92411-1.

University of Alberta Sexual Assault Centre http://psychcentral.com/lib/2008/what-is-a-trigger/

Wade, N.G., Worthington Jr. E.L., and Vogel, D.L. (2007). Effectiveness of religiously tailored interventions in Christian therapy. *Psychotherapy Research.*17:91–105.

Walker, D.F., Reid, H.W., O'Neill, T., & Brown, L. (2009). Changes in personal religion/spirituality during recovery from childhood abuse: A review and synthesis. *Psychological Trauma: Theory, Research, Practice and Policy*, 1, 130-145.

Walker, D.F., Reese, J.B., Hughes, J.P., & Troskie, M.J. (2010). Addressing religious and spiritual issues in trauma focused-Cognitive Behaviour Therapy for children and Adolescents. *Professional Psychology: Research and Practice*. 41(2). 174-180. DOI: 10.1037/a0017782

Webb, M., and Otto Whitmer, K.J. 2003. Parental religiosity, abuse history and maintenance of beliefs taught in the family. *Mental Health, Religion & Culture*. 6(3). 229-239.

CPSIA information can be obtained
at www.ICGtesting.com
Printed in the USA
LVOW04s1526181217
560171LV00011B/373/P